20
/18

RISING ABOVE THE

FLAMES

MY UNTOLD STORY

RISING ABOVE THE FLAMES

MY UNTOLD STORY

JULIE ROWE
AS TOLD TO ERIC J. SMITH

spring creek
BOOK COMPANY
Rexburg, Idaho

ISBN: 978-1-944657-08-6
e. 1

Published by:
Spring Creek Book Company
P.O. Box 1013
Rexburg, Idaho 83440

www.springcreekbooks.com

Cover design © Spring Creek Book Company

Printed in the United States of America
Printed on acid-free paper

TABLE OF CONTENTS

ACKNOWLEDGMENTS

Father in Heaven - Wisdom and intelligence to surpass all understanding.

Jesus Christ - Risked all and gained all.

The Holy Ghost - Testator of truth.

Jeffery Rowe - Strong, valiant, and dedicated.

Melissa Smith - Constant companion.

Chad Daybell - Steadfast and stalwart.

INTRODUCTION

BY ERIC J. SMITH

In the summer of 2014 my sister introduced me to a book called *A Greater Tomorrow* by Julie Rowe. I had recently read another near-death experience book and enjoyed it, despite the high emotions it put my wife and me through. While I believed the author's depictions of future events were authentic, I was particularly troubled by his description of a future plague that would reach the United States.

At the time my sister suggested Julie's book, I hadn't yet resolved my helplessness against contracting plague if it were to arrive on my doorstep. Processing all of the emotion that came with reading such accounts of the future, made me apprehensive to commit to reading a book that I believed might be another emotional roller-coaster.

My wife, on the other hand, was ready for more and accepted Julie's book. After a few chapters, she read a single paragraph aloud concerning a future gathering, which I immediately recognized as a potential way of avoiding the plague and other calamities. A peaceful feeling came over me, and I began to feel confidence in the Lord's plan, and knew He had prepared a way to minimize future heartache to those who heed his warning servants. I asked my wife to start from the beginning of the book reading aloud, and within a few paragraphs I knew I was reading something important for me and my family.

Years later Julie became the subject of interest in major media outlets. I found myself in prayer asking if there were something I could do to relieve her burden and help people to understand her true nature.

Before long and through some peculiar orchestration, I found myself in contact with her and had become the recorder of the Greater Tomorrow Relief Fund. On September 13, 2016 she and I began a series of phone interviews that were initiated to record GTRF business, as well as Julie's understanding of future events that had not been documented in her published books. Those interviews helped establish a relationship of trust that lead to the writing of this book, and other projects.

Through the course of our many interviews and visits, Julie has become one of my and my wife's dearest friends. She has told me many times that I've seen her at her best and at her worst. I therefore consider it a responsibility and privilege to stand as a witness of her genuine compassionate nature, of her bright and very well functioning intellect, and of the gifts she possesses (see 1st Corinthians 12 and 14), some of which I hope to show in these pages.

The doctrinally ignorant culture of our day largely scoffs the idea of spiritual gifts and anyone who claims to have them, especially those who raise a warning voice. I hope the experiences from Julie's life depicted in this book will cause her readers to recognize and feel her genuine heart, and to begin to develop the sense that she is being obedient to a divine call in sharing her message with the world.

"Voices of warning are meant to be heard, not just raised."
Neal A. Maxwell, "Brightness of Hope"; October 1994.

CHAPTER ONE

The Bryan Hyde Show

On May 5, 2016, I was asked by a popular radio talk show host in Southern Utah to be a guest speaker on his show. Bryan Hyde had read my first book, *A Greater Tomorrow*, and was in the process of reading my second book, *The Time is Now*. He was interested in my story, and I was excited to be on his show.

I had finished the first phase of my eighteen-month speaking mission almost a year previously. During those eighteen months I traveled to specific locations where I was invited to speak, and where the spirit told me to go. While most people knew of me through my books and my near-death experience, I was told not to focus on that so much, but was specifically told to focus my message on my witness of the Savior and Heavenly Father's Plan of Happiness. When I made my last public appearance in July of 2015, I had the impression that I was done speaking publicly. I guess the spirit wanted to teach me to "never say never."

The radio interview came at a time when thousands of people in the emergency planning and preparedness communities were anxious to see some of the long anticipated events and prophecies from a number of individuals like me to become fulfilled. Most people in those circles thought an earthquake in Utah would have happened before then, so bloggers and social media pages were hopping with comments and discussion in anticipation of an announcement from me on an impending earthquake.

As I anticipated Bryan's radio talk show I was told to focus on the same message I had given during my speaking events, which I did. I also recounted some of the health challenges I faced that led up to my 2004 near-death experience and some of the things I experienced during that event. I spoke of the current state of things in the nation's politics as well as the spiritual warfare that was going on largely unnoticed.

All of those things led up to a conversation about the Wasatch Wakeup. That phrase was given to me in 2013. I knew it had significance to those on the other side of the veil as being a necessary event that would provide a spiritual shaking, more than a physical shaking, as a sort of final call from heaven to get our lives in order. In the preceding weeks the spirit had been giving me new insights and direction with a new level of intense emotion concerning that future event.

I had seen it repeatedly over the years through vision and dream, I suppose as their way of keeping it fresh in my mind so I could speak and warn about it. Given the state of things on the political landscape at that time, along with the time of year and other circumstances, I felt that the time had come to be more forthright in warning others of the things I understood would soon come to pass.

Often when people ask me questions or share stories it opens my spiritual view to whatever it is they are discussing and I get visuals to varying degrees of intensity. As Bryan asked me questions about the Wasatch Wakeup, it triggered me into a state of vision and I was able to quickly recall the details. Here is what I told him and the rest of the world:

"Yes. I see a full, sunny day with relatively warm weather, actually a little bit unseasonably warm, and then kind of a late night, middle of the night, last minute cold front coming in where

they don't even really give a warning because it's 3 in the morning, people are asleep. There's a little bit of snow, and I see wet snow, so that the morning that people are awakened when the sun comes up after the aftershocks on that initial shake, about 6, 6:30 and people start coming outside in their robes and pajamas, kind of freaked out and they look to survey the damage in their areas, homes and neighborhoods.

I see green grass, like a fresh, spring green grass, the roads are wet, there's been no plowing, it's wet roads and the grass is wet - not from frost, it's wet from melting snow and rain, and then small patches of melting snow would be outside of the snow being water and wet. Very, very wet snow, barely turned to snow, most of it is rain and I don't even remember seeing sleet, it's not icy like that so much.

Then there's of course aftershocks and things like that. That's the initial wake up. We're talking, not this year but later on, an off the charts 9, 9.5, 10 earthquake that will come later. This one is literally a wake up in the morning, and aftershocks for a couple days initially and then here and there throughout the next year or so."

"Imminent"

Following the interview, I was told that chat rooms, web forums, and text messages exploded with conversation. I had announced that the Wasatch Wakeup was "imminent." My word choice created a ripple effect that would come back to bite me for years, but I stand by what I said. The spirit gave me those words, and I obeyed. Still, for the time being everything seemed to be falling in to place. Earthquakes had been picking up in frequency and intensity that week. There was political unrest in the world and talk of riots in Chicago, and the conditions just seemed perfect for the Wasatch Wakeup to happen.

Three days went by without an earthquake. Another two weeks and still there had been no earthquake. Many who believed in my experiences began to feel confused, and began to doubt my gifts and experiences altogether. I knew of some individuals who had invested a significant amount in emergency supplies who began to have regrets and started selling some of their investments.

I didn't have a lot of time to watch the public's reaction because we were in the process of moving from Iowa to Kansas. By the time I had packed, moved, and unpacked at our new house it was August of 2016 and I was left slightly bewildered myself that the earthquake never came. Still, I knew what I had been shown, and despite some of the negative backlash, I knew the Wasatch Wakeup was still imminent. I was told several things by the Spirit that summer regarding the timing of things as it pertained to my mission, and was reminded often that we were "right on track."

CHAPTER TWO

---❖---

My Family History

I am the second child of Don and Janene Hanchett (pronounced han-sit). My father was born in a set of fraternal twins on October 25, 1946 in Safford, Arizona. He is a direct descendant of Edmond Ellsworth, a notable Mormon Pioneer who was in the first handcart company led by Brigham Young, the second president of The Church of Jesus Christ of Latter-day Saints who came westward from Nauvoo in the 1840s. Most of my family lines dating back to the early 1800s are Mormon pioneers are registered in the Daughters of the Utah Pioneers records, and are mentioned in the LDS Church archives.

My Hanchett line runs strong in European history, with mostly English and Scandinavian roots. Some lines in the medieval ages, roughly twenty generations ago, are rich in French Royalty between the 1100s and the 1400s. The royal Hanchett ancestry is a source of great family pride among living descendants.

My father lived in the Safford area until he was seven years of age when his father, Garth, took a job in the San Diego, California area. They would live in that region until my grandpa Garth's death from kidney failure in 1983. His wife, Mae Owens, would live on for another 25 years as a widow, often living with family members. Gram and I had a close relationship, due in part to our shared gifts. She was one of the only people I could ever talk openly with about my dreams and visions, and we would often share our insights together. She has a tender place in my heart to this day, and I miss her very much.

My mother was also born as a twin. Janene Newman was born on August 2, 1948 in Ogden, Utah to Robert and Susan Newman. The Newmans had a long history of living in the United States with a large number of ancestors who crossed the Atlantic Ocean on the Mayflower, and mainly had their roots in England and Scandinavia.

When my mother and aunt were only four days old, my grandma Susan died of hemorrhaging from a stroke. It left my grandpa incapable of providing for his five children on his own. He continued to care for the three older children, and for the first fifteen months of the babies' lives they were provided for by my Aunt Verde and Uncle John, who cared for them as if they were their own children. When mother was fifteen months old grandpa remarried a woman named Stensa Sorenson, who had two children of her own. They raised their combined family in Ogden.

Stensa had stern rules concerning any mention of Susan's name, which continued throughout their children's lives until her death at the age of 94. Only then as mature adults did the Newman children, now grown up, really begin talking about their birth mother. To this day, my mom still gets emotional from the abandonment and heartache she has experienced throughout her life from losing her mother.

When mom began having her own family, she would take us kids to visit Aunt Verde and Uncle John like they were her own parents. I was pretty young then, but I could always feel a sense of love and warmth coming from them. On one of those visits Uncle John gave me a watch, which I kept for many years, and

I still keep a photo of them in my home. They hold a dear place in my heart.

Mom and Dad had ten children together. Following 26 years of marriage, they divorced in 1994 while I was attending college at Brigham Young University. Their divorce was one of the most painful experiences of my life. From the time I was a little girl I loved my family dearly, and I was so grateful for each of my family members. The difficulty of the divorce and trials that followed caused me great heartache. To this day I am still working through some of the trauma that ensued. There are no words to describe the heartbreak, devastation, and despair I have felt regarding these family matters. It is only through the atonement of Jesus Christ that I have come to understand the higher purposes of these trials. It is only through Jesus Christ that I have been healed. His love has seen me through it.

Since I was young I have been constantly aware and sensitive to the presence of my ancestors and other spirits. It didn't take many years for me to realize that it was a special gift, even though I didn't call it that at a young age—I just knew I was different from other people. I had a constant awareness of my ancestor's interest in me from my earliest recollections. I have often felt my grandparents' and other ancestors' presence and am so thankful for their love and compassion.

I've learned that when I get visuals, hear voices, receive impressions, and feel directed to do or say certain things it is because they are giving me those things. Because of their continual nearness and regular messages, I often give them credit as I know they are working under the direction of the spirit in my life. I recognize they are working under the directives of Father in Heaven who bestows my blessings and revelations.

They've made it known to me that I am a descendant of John the Revelator through the Davidic Line, as well as some other scriptural figures. They've also shown me my father's French ancestry which includes the family of Joan of Arc, who I have always felt a deep connection with. I have memories pertaining to Joan and have been shown that she and I have many similarities. Our missions have an interesting parallel which will become more evident in years to come, and I love that we share the same birthday!

The messages they've given me regarding my ancestry are not always good. They've shown me that one of my French ancestors was an unrighteous king who tortured some individuals, sent them to prison, and cruelly caused them to be dismembered. In other scenes I knew of incest, and the abuse of family and servants. Having seen some of those things, it pains me that we still have some in the family line on the other side of the veil who have chosen to follow the adversary.

In that spirit, I enjoy doing family history work and I'm not ashamed to discover the true stories of my family's past. I do it with the intent that I might help to open and heal their hearts, that they might find forgiveness of their wrongs and not only turn their hearts to their children, but hopefully help them turn their hearts to Christ. This is one of the many reasons I enjoy the work I do as an energy practitioner.

My great-great-grandfather Edmund Ellsworth,
a notable Mormon Pioneer who was in the first handcart company
led to the Rocky Mountains by Brigham Young in the 1840s.

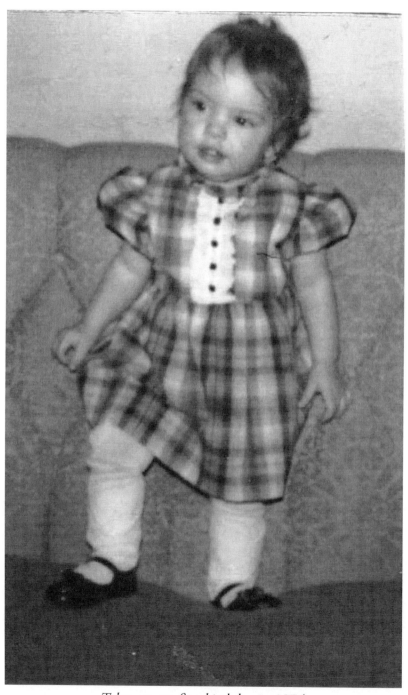

Taken on my first birthday in 1974.

CHAPTER THREE

A Rough Start

In the summer of 1972, my mom and dad were in a motorcycle accident. My mom was two months pregnant with me. Dad took her to the hospital where medical staff found that my heartbeat had stopped. Mom asked dad to give her a priesthood blessing. For two and a half weeks they could find no heartbeat.

Ultrasound technology was not common at the time, so without a heartbeat it was advised that the baby be aborted. Still feeling hope, my mom asked for another blessing and that they attempt to find a heart beat one last time before proceeding with the abortion procedure. After much fasting and prayer and another blessing, miraculously the heart beat returned, and the procedure was cancelled. My mom spent the rest of her pregnancy on bed rest, with some physical struggles including hemorrhaging.

I was born on January 6, 1973, just at the expected time. My parents named me Julie Kay Hanchett. I was fully developed, but weighed a meager 4 pounds, 13 ounces. My mom told me my body was the size of a baby bottle. The doctors' explanation for my tininess was that the placenta had detached during the trauma of the motorcycle accident, and had later reattached in a more cramped space. Therefore the placenta had not reached its full capacity and restricted my growth.

My parents initially felt some concern for my size, but within a few months, my chubby cheeks were evidence that I had recovered from any physical trauma that may have occurred. I believe part of my sensitivity to the veil comes from my traumatic experience in the womb.

It appeared that I was in great physical condition, but even as an infant I had incurred some emotional trauma through the experience. In about 2014, I was drawn to the discipline of energy healing, and became engaged in a number of energy healing sessions. Through those experiences it became apparent that some of the physical and emotional ailments I had been experiencing as an adult had ties to the emotional trauma of my entrance to the world nearly forty years previously.

Some of the emotions that came up during those sessions were panic, fear, anger, and grief. Through those healing sessions I recognized that the adversary wanted me to believe that the emotion of fear was caused by not believing I was good enough, or capable of completing my mission, and that my life on earth would be too difficult to possibly make it back home.

I came to see through those adversarial doubts that the true message concerning my fear was that I might not be able to come to earth and fulfill my mission, and that perhaps the adversary had accomplished his purpose in thwarting it. I came to understand that the devil's twisted tactics are used to cause men and women to downplay their worth, to win mankind over to their side, and that those tactics often begin at a young age. I recall at an early age hearing the adversary say, "See, you didn't even want to come to earth."

Or they would tell me how weak I was, or how difficult my life would be. They tried to get me to believe that I would have been better off choosing to reject Heavenly Father's plan to come to earth in the way they had rejected it. I came to see those messages were attempts to try to persuade me early on that I was not special, and had no important reason for living. But I found that those messages were often countered by my heavenly helpers who would show me the importance of my role on earth, and my mission. The Lord often teaches me through contrasts of dark and light.

I have been blessed with a good memory since I was young. When I was about eighteen months old, we lived in Midway, Utah, and my mom had a teaching job that required putting me and two of my siblings in daycare. On her way to work she would drop us off with a neighbor who ran a childcare business out of her home.

I still remember the details of that place. The care provider had long light brown hair which she often wore in a pony tail, or straight down her back and kind of messy. There were four to eight other children. I remember the location of the bathroom, and recall one of those popular 1970s oval-shaped braided rugs with concentric rings in the middle of the floor. There was a big rocking chair, and I can still see the toys, their shapes, and colors.

I remember the dishonesty of the woman with my mom. She said we were free to go anywhere we liked in her home, but then she restricted our activities to a certain room after mom left. One day I was playing with a particular toy, when the caretaker grabbed my older sister and beat her to the point she received several bruises on her back. I can still describe where those bruises were inflicted, and the deep emotions I felt. It was horrible!

Shortly after that, my family moved to Texas due to a military assignment my father had been given. About a year later at the age of three I remember my parents put me down for a nap. They taught me that jumping on the bed was inappropriate, but on that day I was bored and chose to do so anyway. I remember jumping up and down as quietly as I could on my bed having a great time. After a few minutes I laid back down and my dad came in and said, "Julie, were you jumping on the bed?"

I told him "no." Again he pressed on, and said "Julie, are you telling the truth?"

I was silent. After a few minutes I confessed. My dad then told me to bend over his knee and he smacked my bottom. He sat me on his knee and gave me a quick lesson.

After I shed some tears my dad explained the importance of telling the truth and what a lie was. He hugged me and told me he loved me. I resolved then and there to always try to be honest, and I promised him I would not lie to him. To this day, whenever I am faced with a decision to be dishonest I remember the time I jumped on my bed and lied about it, and my dad's important lesson.

On another occasion I was outside playing with my older sister on a teeter totter, when she suddenly felt nature calling. About the time she reached the back door, a brown bird flew down and landed on my head. The bird stayed there for three to four minutes, as my mother watched with fascination from the back door.

Before the bird landed, I had been given a visual of the bird doing just what it had done, flying down from the tree and landing right on top of my head. When it happened I was amazed, and remember thinking, "How did I know that was going to happen? Am I magic?"

I remember having a sort of conversation with the bird in my mind. Then I began to feel a little afraid, but I felt a voice whispering to me repeatedly, "It's okay. It just likes you."

I had thoughts of magical Disney princesses who could speak to animals and I wondered if I had similar magical princess powers. The experience overall was actually very spiritual for me, and I didn't just view it as a silly coincidence.

Later on I asked my mom why that had happened to me. She said that perhaps the bird just thought my hair looked like a nest. From then on a few of my siblings teased me saying that I had "nest hair." The adversary followed up their teasing by telling me it was nothing more than a silly little bird landing in my "nest hair." From an early age the devil has tried to minimize special experiences and gifts of the spirit.

I was able to discern truth from error from early on. I remember one of my elementary school teachers saying that "rocks are inanimate objects." Right away I sensed a voice explaining to me that it was a false statement, because I had often felt the energy of rocks and their similarity to animals and other living things, and I had even sensed some measure of communication with them. But by that time I knew I couldn't convey those thoughts with other people because I knew they wouldn't believe me.

I was sensitive to the comments and thoughts of children from early on. One time when I was four years old my mom was reading a book to me on her lap, and she told me I was her "miracle baby," and how she and my dad thought they would lose me. Satan used this to tell me things like "You have a small brain," or "You're stupid."

I often heard the adversary tell me I was ugly and deformed. I already knew my spiritual gifts made me different, but the constant onslaught of negative voices brought heart pain and insecurity, and had an impact on my young heart.

After living in Fort Hood for three years, my dad received a new assignment, requiring him to serve one year unaccompanied by family in Germany. My mom had four children at the time and we stayed with my aunt whose husband was out of town for six months doing sales. She had six children so combined with my family, my mom and aunt had their hands full.

One day my cousin brought the chicken pox home from

school, which then went through all ten of us children. It was a period of high anxiety for my mom, whose husband was away, and who had the stress of ten children living in a home that was not her own, living in a state far from their last home, all on top of a houseful of itchy, needy children.

My young heart must have felt some of the weight my mom carried, when a gray haired woman who I understood to be one of my ancestors on the other side of the veil came to let me know that my mom and the others would be fine.

Our six months in California ended when my dad came home from his assignment. I remember feeling extra happy to see him, but he had grown a mustache. I was surprised and a little shy, because I had never seen him that way before.

My dad was promoted as a Captain in the military and was stationed in Tacoma, Washington. We packed up our motor home and decided to take the scenic route through Utah to see my mom's family on our way to Washington. I was excited for a new adventure but on the other hand, I was really sad to have to leave my cousins.

I loved traveling in our motor home. My parents put me and my sister in the bed that was nearly over the driver's seat where I had a view out the front window. I would gaze through that window for hours. I was usually the last to fall asleep because I enjoyed the scenery so much. I also loved being directly over my parents so I could eavesdrop on their conversations, which I would do for hours while my siblings were asleep.

As we drew closer to Utah, I remember feeling their increased anxiety and stress in their voices. My dad didn't care for Utah, and my mom felt anxiety over rekindling family relationships that had not always brought her a lot of happiness. By listening in on their conversations I gained some deeply personal insights into their lives—things about other family members, things about each other, and other things little girls shouldn't know.

After stopping in Utah I was excited to get to Washington and begin kindergarten. I loved watching Sesame Street and by that time had sufficiently learned my ABC's, colors, shapes, and introductory reading, each of which I had learned largely on my own.

Since I was that age I liked to use either of my hands interchangeably for various activities. For example, I preferred eating and writing with my left hand, and throwing softballs, batting, and other activities with my right hand.

One day a teacher observed my frequent use of the left hand in writing and coloring, so she gave me a pair of green handled scissors that were designed for left-handed and special needs children. I was so frustrated when she assigned the special needs teacher to work with me.

I preferred to use scissors with my right hand, but I didn't have the courage or communication skills to let them know I preferred using normal scissors with my right hand. So as I passed them between both hands to try to find the most comfortable way, my teachers were watching me struggle.

I was skilled at coloring within the lines and even knew how to blend colors to create a more textured appearance, so my teachers were puzzled when they saw how much I struggled with the green scissors. I sensed that my teachers believed that I had special needs.

One day one of my classmates wasn't using his "normal" scissors so I snatched them, quickly finished my cutting job, and completed it before all the other children, and then put them back on his desk. My teachers finally realized I used both my hands, and used them well.

As I grew older I became more comfortable and confident in my gifts, even though I still didn't think of them as gifts; I just knew I was a little different. I began seeing people, places, and other situations that were new to me that felt like they were from the past, which I would later recognize as pre-mortal memories. I also began having visions of things that felt futuristic that I would later realize were visions of future events.

We would often go on Sunday drives to enjoy eastern Washington's beautiful mountains, volcanoes, and scenic forests. Some of the sites we visited included Mount St. Helens, and Mount Rainier. Exposure to geographic places like that often gave me context that would lead to visionary insight.

For example, in May of 1980 I had a precursory visionary experience of the Mount St. Helens eruption. Only days before Helens erupted, I had a vision and felt a sort of rumbling in the air while playing in my backyard. The related theme of those separate experiences combined to give me an unsettled feeling that something was going to happen. When Mount St. Helens did erupt, it validated my impressions from days before. Through that and other experiences I felt like I was being taught how my gifts worked.

I remember on another occasion driving near Mount Rainier and asking my dad if that mountain had erupted, or if it was going to erupt soon. I had seen it erupting like Mount St. Helens, but to this day, Mount Rainier has still not exploded. Incidentally, I continue to have dreams of the mountain erupting and believe it won't be much longer before the dreams, visions, and rumbling sensations I felt as a child come to pass.

As with other visuals like those, I knew when Mount St. Helens exploded that I had seen it beforehand, but I didn't feel like I had anyone to talk with. I wanted very badly to let others know what I was experiencing, but I had learned so many times prior that sharing such experiences always fell on unwelcoming ears, and that when I did try to share it would only lead to my sadness.

Being so young, my siblings weren't in a state of being able to comprehend what I was experiencing, so I learned to keep those things to myself and my Heavenly Father in prayer. I did have one church leader at that age who I felt would have believed me, but the opportunity to speak to him never presented itself.

In second grade, I had my tonsils and adenoids removed, which required a stay in the hospital. The nurses began with a shot and some laughing gas to numb my senses, and then the medical staff wheeled me off to the procedure room with my parents walking beside me.

As they walked with me I clearly remember the peculiar sensation of floating up and having a direct view of my body beneath me, as well as the doctors and nurses who were carrying out their various responsibilities. I have come to think of that event as my first out-of-body experience.

Then when I was at home recovering I remember hearing music by angelic voices, which I would later recognize came from the other side of the veil. I also heard the voice I understood to be a distant grandmother ministering to me and telling me I would be okay. I was sick in bed for a week, and then went back to school.

About that time I was having a number of experiences of connecting with animals. Washington's humid climate created the right conditions for having green tree frogs in our backyard, which I liked to catch with my siblings. We did that often and a number of times I would sense when it was time to put the frog down, as if the little creatures were asking me to stop playing with them.

Sometimes my brothers didn't get that sense, so I would ask them to put the frogs down. I knew their overplaying led to the frog's discomfort. In essence, my brothers "loved them to death," which made my heart feel deep sympathy for the little frogs.

My parents kept rabbits as a protein source for our family. We would keep them for six weeks and then butcher them. I begged my parents to let me watch the butchering. I was curious, and I wanted to know what happened in the cellar. But my mom said I was too young to watch the bunnies to be butchered.

However, one day my dad took his friend and me to the cellar to butcher one of the rabbits. He used a hammer to the back of the animal's head, knocking it unconscious. He then butchered the rabbit, and proceeded to give me an anatomy lesson as he divided and skinned the animal. I cried for weeks following the experience. I felt the emotions of that little rabbit and it broke my heart.

We had a German Shepherd named Barron. One day my brother took Barron down a slide which led to an accident breaking Barron's leg. It crippled him for the remainder of his life. I felt tremendous heartbreak over the experience, and could feel our dog calling out in pain and suffering. After moving to Hawaii, Barron died of a broken heart, having never fully recovered from the fall. Once again it seemed I could feel the animal's emotions.

Our backyard had a great clubhouse, where my siblings and friends became self identified as the "Pigs in Space" club. I didn't like the name because I didn't like being called a pig. One Sunday the neighborhood boys came by and stole the toads in the backyard near the clubhouse and sold them back to my brothers for a dollar each. They were the same trouble maker neighbor kids who would throw apples at us from their backyard apple tree. I didn't like the way those boys made me feel.

It was while living in Washington that I learned about haunted houses. At the age of six I had a babysitter who read a ghost story before bed, and then told me our house was haunted. As she read the story and spoke of the ghosts, I remember them coming right into the home, just like they were invited in. I threw a temper tantrum, and wouldn't go to sleep.

When my parents came home I tried to explain what I was experiencing amid my tantrum. But in an effort to stop my rebellion they spanked me, told me I had been a bad girl and not to act out like that again. They made me apologize to the babysitter. In my view at the time, my dad was more concerned with my tantrum and the embarrassment I had caused the family than my feelings and the experience I had with evil spirits.

At about that time I discovered that I had an unusual sense of respect for nature. There was a forest behind our home that provided a good location for cutting down Christmas trees. I remember feeling peculiar sadness when my dad brought the freshly chopped tree into the home. I realized that it was the sadness of the tree itself that I felt—a sadness that communicated its sorrow for being cut down unnecessarily. But then I remember feeling the tree's emotions improve as it became decorated and found a useful purpose again.

It was also in Washington that I learned about some of the impure intentions of other kids. One night my parents went on a date and hired a sixth-grade boy from my school to come babysit for a couple hours. When he arrived I had an uneasy feeling about him, and was warned by the spirit to be cautious around him. At those times I was near him I could sense that he was looking at me inappropriately.

Just as I left the school grounds the next day on my one-mile walk home I heard someone call out, "Hey Julie." When I turned to look toward the voice I found the same boy who had babysat me the night previously facing me with his pants down. It was my first exposure, and first sexual assault, and I understood why the spirit had given me the caution to be careful around him.

I went home and told my mom what had happened, which made her upset. My dad was a Captain in the military and had been away on business that day so mom waited for dad to come home before confronting the boys' parents.

Things got complicated when my parents realized the boy's father was a Major and held rank over my dad. It was a time when my dad was concerned with his rank, pay, and livelihood as a military officer. About a week later we went to the boy's home to confront him but he wasn't home. I nervously recounted what took place to his mother without him or his father present. I was devastated when the mother replied, "This is not a big deal. Boys will be boys."

I went home and cried. I felt rejected and abused, and knew justice had not been served.

My first grade teacher, Mrs. Johnson, played a significant role in teaching me how unkind some people can be. In the classroom she regularly told children to "shut up," which was like using a swear word in my home. Mrs. Johnson was known to hit misbehaving children's hands or the top of their heads with her yardstick. She often threw the chalkboard eraser across the room striking misbehaving children in the head.

One special needs boy often wet his pants in class, and Mrs. Johnson grew tired of dealing with it, so she sent him to the back of the room to sit on the tiled portion of the floor. In an effort to teach him to control himself, she did not let him go to the restroom, to the point he would wet himself at the back of the room. I was sensitive to the feelings of alienation and embarrassment Mrs. Johnson had created for him, and it broke my heart.

That came at an age I would later come to understand that I was an "empath," meaning I can feel other people's emotions and have a tendency to absorb the negative emotions around me like a sponge. Negativity doesn't just get absorbed and then disappear; rather, any kind of negative emotion I take in has a way of manifesting itself through illness and pain until it gets released. It is a process I have learned to work through, and I have spent hundreds and hundreds of hours in my adulthood releasing the negative emotions I have absorbed.

I felt so sorry for that boy in class and wanted to help him so badly that only in my adulthood have I come to realize the effect Mrs. Johnson's disciplinary style had on me. My heart was broken for him and the way he was treated, and the negative emotions I took in contributed to some recurring nightmares in my life for many years.

Mrs. Johnson's negative disposition had a terrifying effect on me. It caused me to get sick with anxiety in anticipation of going to school each morning. After about a month of having an upset stomach and dreading going to school, my mom sent my 6'6" father to the parent teacher conference to put a little fear in Mrs. Johnson. Following his visit she was a little more kind and didn't bother me for the remainder of the school year. She was fired a year later.

My most memorable experience from second grade was when I was baptized on January 12, 1981, six days following my eighth birthday. When my bishop called me in for an interview, I was deeply touched by the spirit and remember crying.

In my next year of school there were an unusually high number of third graders. The teachers had to get creative in order to handle the imbalance of students. They recognized that I was performing ahead of my class and placed me in the fourth grade for part of the time.

During that school year we learned sign language, which came naturally to me. I always held a tender place in my heart for deaf people and had the hope of being able to speak to them through signing one day.

That was about the time I began to realize some of the conniving tendencies of some kids. That school year I had two popular friends named Summer and April. What started out as a good friendship with the two girls began to change over an incident with the boys. The girls gradually became best friends and started leaving me out of their activities. A clash began one day when the boys came to me and said, "April and Summer are cute, but they don't know how to play soccer." It felt nice to have my athletic ability appreciated!

Most girls spent their recess time walking around, doing kartwheels, and gossiping about people. I thought people should be kind, and that behavior bugged me. I began to notice that with some people the nicer I was to them, the less kind they treated me.

At that age I began realizing my sensitivity to the thoughts, emotions, and discussions others would have behind my back. For example, I could sense their conversations concerning the clothing people wore, their braces, glasses, their special needs, or the nerdy comments they made in class. I didn't know why they would talk about those things. Looking back I can see their unkind treatment toward me or others was probably jealousy, but I wasn't really sure why. I had issues with my self esteem and didn't feel pretty, so I can only attribute their jealousy to the way I kindly treated others.

As an empath, negative and backstabbing conversation from others always had a negative effect on me. I thought their girlish games were boring anyway, so it became a turning point in my life as I began to realize my natural shoe-in with the boys and lessening interests in many of the typical girlish activities and tendencies. To this day I struggle with catty, back-stabbing girls, and I can trace it back to this age. I feel like the root of gossip is in the insecurities of those who are doing it, and the fruits of gossip are destruction for everybody involved.

I have sometimes wondered about my less natural fit with girls and more comfortable match with boys. I've always had a strong sense of sobriety that I think has often intimidated my girl friends. I found that most boys just played hard and engaged very little in chit chat which naturally drew me to them.

When I was in third grade for about half of the school year, my dad was accepted in chaplaincy school, which took our family on a six-month stint to New Jersey. As with all of our moves, I cried when we left Washington. My only solace was in knowing that our good friends, the Breinholts, would also be stationed there. They were a large military family like ours and had also been stationed in Washington. They had a son my age named Chuck, and a daughter named Emily who were dear friends, so knowing I would have good friends through the move made everything better.

On our journey east we stopped to spend some time with my mom's family in Utah. As an LDS chaplain in the military, my dad was privileged to work with the Quorum of the Twelve Apostles and the First Presidency of the Church of Jesus Christ of Latter-day Saints. Two times a year he spent a couple weeks meeting with them at the church office building. My Grandpa Hanchett also had his own connection with the brethren, serving with Spencer W. Kimball in a Stake Presidency in Arizona a number of years previously.

My dad and grandfather's close connections provided an opportunity for our entire family to meet with President Kimball, who was at that time serving as the President of the church. We met him in his office, where he gave each of us kids a picture of the Savior and a picture of himself, and then he spent some time speaking about various doctrines of the gospel.

Among those topics he discussed the Native Americans and the important role they would play in the Last Days. I'll never forget the way President Kimball looked directly into my eyes as he spoke of the latter days.

It was a validating experience for me because I had been having dreams and visions of being in the prophet's office before we arrived. One thing I remember from those experiences was seeing a chief Indian headdress on the bookshelf of his office. I was delighted when I actually saw it there in real life, and was even more delighted when President Kimball took the headdress down and let my little brother put it on.

After about thirty minutes, President Kimball shook each of our hands and said goodbye. He died in November of 1985, about a year after our visit. I cried for weeks after his funeral, but I remember the way the spirit comforted me and witnessed to my heart that Spencer W. Kimball was a true prophet of God. Having just become a baptized member of the church only weeks before, it was an experience that had a lasting impact upon my young heart, and I have cherished it ever since. Because of the lasting impression he had on me, my husband Jeff and I named our second son, Spencer, after him.

After visiting President Kimball, I found myself on my Grandpa Newman's knee just before departing Utah to New Jersey. As he spoke to me I received visuals of him shoveling snow and falling down. The spirit let me know that grandpa would soon be dying but not to be afraid; that my mother would be getting on an airplane to attend the funeral with her family, and that I needed to be a strong girl and help my brothers and sisters. It was the last time I saw him in this life. Three days later on New Year's Day grandpa was shoveling snow so they could go to church, which led to his fatal cardiac arrest. Since we had already started driving to New Jersey at the time of grandpa's funeral, my mother flew back west, just as I had been told.

Most of our time in New Jersey was spent on the military base, but we were able to get out and do some site seeing once in awhile. I remember going into the city, and seeing homeless people, the Statue of Liberty, Time Square, Ellis Island, and some other popular attractions. But of all my experiences there, my favorite memory was of attending the Barnum and Bailey Circus!

By that time I had read about men being shot out of cannons, breathing fire, and I had dreams of one day becoming a lion tamer and a trapeze artist. One night I had a dream of attending the circus events beforehand. On March 31, 1982, my mom packed up her six children, along with Mrs. Breinholt and her children, and we boarded the New York Subway and headed into the big city for the show. I've always thought it was so brave, and perhaps a little risky, that my mom did that, but I also think it was very cool.

I loved the circus, but I was sensitive to the emotions of the animals and couldn't help feeling sorry for each of them, especially the elephants and lions. Each time they were whipped I felt their pain and wanted to set them all free.

The only time I have ever been to New York City was during those six months. I had seen it several times in movie scenes and later in life when I lived in nearby Washington D.C. I had numerous opportunities to stay with friends there. I also had some professional opportunities to go there, but I never desired to. I have seen New York City many times in dream and vision, though.

In February of 2017 while writing this chapter, I had a dream where I was a child visiting New York City again, which caused me to consider all that had happened since that time nearly thirty years ago. My dream flashed forward to the future and I saw myself on television there, visiting the New York Temple, and the U.N. building following an earthquake in Utah.

In that dream I sensed a new message and the Lord's voice saying, "You're coming full circle." I felt gratitude for His wisdom and mercy allowing me to visit the Big Apple one last time before a major change would take place there.

While living in New Jersey, I was in the third grade and became friends with a girl named Stephanie. She decided she liked my friend, Chuck Breinholt, who had been my boyfriend since kindergarten. This did not sit well with me. For Chuck's birthday his family held a social event at the roller skating rink.

I knew Stephanie was fully aware of my interest in Chuck,

which made me all the more upset when the snowball song came up and Chuck asked Stephanie to hold hands and skate around the rink with him. I felt an energy that came like a dagger to my heart, pierced with anger and jealousy. As Chuck and Stephanie skated off, he turned around and shouted to me, "You can come too; you can come hold my other hand." I stubbornly shouted "No!" and said to myself, "I will never hold hands with a boy who holds hands with another girl."

Our time in New Jersey ended when my dad was promoted to a Major in the army, and was reassigned to Hawaii. That move was especially tough because it meant parting ways with the Breinholts and my friend Chuck. I cried for weeks. Before taking our next post in Hawaii we stayed with family in Utah and California for a few months. By that time I was aware of many of my gifts and had developed strong interests in things I liked and things I didn't care for so much.

Age 2 in 1975 in Midvale, Utah.

First grade photo in Washington state.

CHAPTER FOUR

Increasing Gifts in a Tropical Paradise

While living in Hawaii, we were stationed at Schofield Barracks in the city of Wahiawa on the island of Oahu. I was initially a little apprehensive leaving the mainland and everything I was familiar with, but the apprehension didn't last long when I realized how much fun we would have on the beaches and all that would come from living in a tropical paradise.

My Hawaiian school experience was unique, rewarding, and diverse. I spent my time in Hawaii playing soccer with the boys, just like back in Washington, but I also played kickball, marbles, and arm wrestling with them. I beat those boys in everything, except I could never quite defeat two of them at arm wrestling. I also spent my recess time with a few girls playing Japanese jump rope and four square.

My educational experiences while in Hawaii were a major catalyst for enhancing some of my spiritual gifts. As my teachers discussed historical figures and events, many times the events and people were played out before me in real time. Through those lessons I developed an unusually strong connection with historical figures like Queen Isabella who funded Christopher

Columbus' voyage to the Americas, Joan of Arc, Pocahontas, and Anne Frank, to name a few. As I read Anne's diary I feel an uncanny familiarity with her expressions, interests, and even her hand writing.

While living on the Island I learned to play some of the traditional musical instruments, made poi balls, and I took Hula lessons from a neighbor. I loved learning how to make lei's. My family was active and frequently went swimming at the beach and enjoyed site seeing together. We also enjoyed going to a few local swimming pools on a regular basis.

In fourth grade I had long straight hair, but by fifth grade I wore orthodontic headgear, glasses, and had short hair. My glasses were the cause of ridicule from other kids who called me "four-eyes," but I wasn't bullied like some of the other kids. Bullying made me mad. Whenever I saw abuse in any way from other kids I tried to offer help to those who needed it.

I began recognizing that popular kids were not always kind to others, and that the best way to get along with others was to be genuine and kind. Bullying became a major focus of my platform when I ran for Class Representative in fourth grade, which I won. It was a good boost to my social life.

My dad worked as an informal liaison for the LDS church and the military by helping to coordinate tours to the LDS Polynesian Cultural Center for military families at a discount. We went there often, and I remember the recently released Johnny Lingo, a popular short LDS film featuring islanders and the journey of a woman the village considered to be homely, who became beautiful in the end because of the way Johnny treated her. I even got to meet a number of cast members on one of our visits.

One of my most memorable experiences of the fourth grade came when our class took a week-long field trip to The Big Island. It was a privilege none of my other siblings had while we lived in Hawaii. Oahu was a thirty minute flight from the Big Island. Our field trip had a rough start. There was a kid named Eddie, who had a crush on me. He wanted to sit by me on the plane. I let him, not really wanting to, but I knew I might be able to have a positive impact on him. I had noticed how he was bullied by kids and I felt bad for him. I spent the flight listening to him and tried to make him feel special. When we reached our destination we went to the KOA lodge where we stayed for the week.

By that time, I had become acquainted with some of the traditions and cultural background of the Hawaiian Islands. Over the next five days my spiritual gifts became heightened and more frequent. I was having night and day visions, and out of body experiences on subjects related to the Island's past and future. For example, our tour led along a path to a garden lava area inundated with totem poles and a dark history. I sensed a deep sort of wickedness emanating from the totem poles, as well as one of the pits that had been preserved from an earlier era of heathen human sacrifice. I felt sick to my stomach.

While standing there I experienced events from long ago in real-time. I saw lines of women, young virgins, and children waiting for their turn, as they were forced into the pit by evil men. I experienced this view as if I were one of the women, and felt their inexpressible horror as we were being forced to jump. Scenes and voices of the deceased souls who were lingering in that location called out, "Help me, help me, help me!"

The scene was so horrific it put me in a state of heightened anxiety, as I experienced a change in breathing, and felt I would pass out. Having slipped from my body twice before, I recognized my spirit began detaching from my body.

In tears and desperation I began to run from the scene as fast as I could, when a man in his early twenties appeared to me and told me things would be okay. I knew my visitor was the spirit form of a man who would be born very soon. He brought a sense of comfort and light to me, but as I was still in a state of panic, I continued running to a place further down the trail where I felt safer. My visitor stayed with me for a little while longer.

For weeks prior to the trip to the Big Island, I had been shown a volcanic blast taking place there. As we continued our tour I began to recognize the landscape of The Big Island matched my dreams. When they told us we would be hiking the crater of Mount Kilauea, I felt scared as I wondered if the eruption I had seen in my dreams would happen; but the spirit whispered to me that I would be okay.

When we were on the crater, I saw it erupt again in real-time through my spiritual eyes. They also taught me about the Hawaiian Volcano Goddess, Pele, and the Heart of Pele, and gave me the understanding that the legends surrounding those myths had significance to my mortal mission.

Kilauea erupted the very next day in January 1983, and it was not coincidental I was there during that rare event. It was the second time I had seen a natural disaster in vision and personally saw its fulfillment.

I found some of the island traditions had interesting truths, such as don't touch Pele's hair, and don't take lava from the island or you'll have bad luck. I didn't believe those legends for the mysteries' sake, but I had always felt like the earth should be respected, and having lived in Hawaiian tropical paradise for three years, my reverence for nature deepened. I felt like nature should be enjoyed, but that it is in its happiest state as it is. I always had a hard time when people littered, or hurt bugs, tree limbs, roots, or even rocks. Even the seemingly harmless act of carving a stick makes me uncomfortable. I began to prefer that nature should be enjoyed, but left alone.

As we continued our tour I experienced a number of similar visuals as with the totem poles, though not quite as intensely, and my spirit continued to slip in and out of my body with each experience. I was also shown visuals of ancient times of war through a first person perspective under the reign of King Kamehameha, which visuals I have never been able to make sense of until recently.

Overall, the deeply emotional experiences I had on the Big Island left me with little desire to return again, but I enjoyed the geographic setting and beautiful scenery very much. As a side note, in May of 2016, I attended a health symposium in Las Vegas, Nevada. While on that business trip I met with some people to discuss my nonprofit organization. One of the men brought his son who was nine years younger than me, and I immediately recognized him as the man who helped me at the totem poles, and who was also tied to the visuals I had of fighting during ancient Hawaiian wars.

In the fifth grade I was chosen as Student Body Vice President, and in sixth grade I was elected Student Body President, winning by a landslide. I recognized that my success was from being genuine, kind, and always giving my heart to others.

My kindness may have been what led a young man named Brad to take me up in a tree one day. He was a popular kid in school and was good at soccer. High up in those branches and away from everyone else he felt comfortable enough to ask me for a kiss. He was cute and I liked him a lot, but I let him know that I couldn't date boys until I was sixteen.

He responded, "It would be between you and me—no one would ever have to know."

I told him my parents said I couldn't date until I was sixteen, and that God would know if I kissed him. He asked at least three more times. I held firm, partly because I sensed a heavenly visitor in the tree with us, and I wasn't about to go against the standards I had been taught. Brad wasn't happy. For the rest of our time in Hawaii, he was very unkind to me, even to the point of bullying me just because I had turned down his affection.

It was about that time that I had been feeling discomfort in my feet from the way my big toes were growing. Medical professionals recommended a surgical procedure that would hopefully straighten my large toe. They felt it would only be necessary on my left foot and would see how things healed before repeating the surgery on the other foot. The procedure was carried out at Tripler Hospital which was 45 minutes away from Schofield Barracks where we lived. It was a tall pink building, and stands to this day.

As with my tonsillectomy back in Washington, the nurses began anesthesia by fastening monitors to my chest, administering laughing gas and a shot. After being fastened to the operation table I looked up at the lights, and then my view shifted as I saw my body lying on the table beneath me with medical staff nearby.

That scene was repeated at another point during the surgical procedure as my spirit left my body again. I have come to think of this as my third out-of-body experience. I remember feeling a little alarmed from the sensation of being out of my body, but having had a similar experience during my tonsillectomy I came to believe that was just what happened during surgical procedures. The surgery helped only slightly, but caused my big left toe to be stunted in growth, which still causes me pain on a regular basis.

Visions at a Young Age

By the time I was eleven, I had experienced a number of visions and dreams of the oceans acting violently. I began to learn through school classes that what I had been shown was called a tsunami. In many of those visuals I had also seen storms, earthquakes, displaced people, and white tents.

In 1982, I began having dreams of high winds and damage on the island where we lived. In the weeks following those dreams, a historic hurricane passed through called Iwa (pronounced "Eva"). It was the final hurricane of significance for the year, and was the largest to hit Hawaii since its statehood in 1959.

According to Wikipedia, Iwa damaged over 2,300 buildings, and left 500 people homeless, and damages exceeded $300 million (1982 USD). It tore the roof right off our carport, and uprooted a large climbing tree in our yard, and left us without power and water for a week. But we were very blessed living on the military base. The same storm left others on the island without running water for up to three weeks.

During my last year in Hawaii, at the age of twelve I entered the Young Women program of the LDS Church. Unlike most girls' camps on the mainland, it was a unique experience to have our activities, tents, and cots right on the beach! We went on a five-mile hike into the Hawaiian mountains on the Island of Oahu. It was an amazing experience! The only downer was the centipedes, cockroaches, and scorpions in the showers.

I had been receiving visions and impressions throughout the week, but had a new experience. There was a girl who I'll call Jenny that was investigating my church, who had come along for the week-long activity. I knew she was sort of a "wild girl," but I tried my best to fellowship and spend time with her.

One night I was awakened by Jenny who was experiencing a demonic possession in our tent. I don't think the other girls knew what was happening, but I could tell she wasn't acting normally and sensed the presence of darkness. I felt a little frightened. I was directed to be bold and command the evil spirit to leave, which happened. It was the first time I had ever done something like that. I felt prompted to bear my witness of Jesus Christ's power and ability to heal, and shared a witness of my faith with her.

On our five-mile hike the next morning, Jenny shared her feelings of the reality and specialness of the experience the night before, which she said "changed her life," and she thanked me sincerely for my role in helping her. I felt like Jenny had also changed my life in the process of helping her.

My upbringing was such that modesty in dress, especially at the beach, was always enforced. I was insecure about my body at that period of time as I had begun experiencing physical changes, at what I now see was a relatively young age. The dress and clothing choices other girls made was often a concern to me. Short shorts and tank tops were the popular attire, but I preferred to wear loose fitting t-shirts, covering up the best I could.

Years later when I was in eighth grade, I stood at about 5'8". College boys and GIs often made advances on me, thinking I was much older than I was. I took great effort to dress modestly and tried not to draw attention to myself through my appearance.

Our three years in Hawaii drew to an end when my dad received a new assignment to work on his MBA at Syracuse University in Upstate New York. It was a required credential if he wanted to continue to advance in his military career. The original plan was to stay in Utah for three weeks and then move to New York together as a family. But things didn't always go as planned.

I was twelve years old when we landed back on the mainland. On our way to Utah we stopped to visit my grandparents, Garth and Mae Hanchett, who were living in San Diego, California. Grandpa Hanchett, who I called "Gramps," was in very poor health, which required that he be on oxygen. He was 6'3" and weighed about 100 lbs. Gramps died two weeks after our visit, just two weeks before his 60th birthday. His premature death left Gram, who was 58 years old at the time, a widow for over 25 years.

A Dark Summer

We stayed with my grandma Newman for the next three weeks in Utah. Then, wanting a more stable lifestyle, my mom tried to convince dad to leave the military and put down roots there. When the time came to go back east, my mom wanted more time with her family, since they had been away from them in Hawaii for so long.

Dad resisted the new plan at first, but eventually agreed to let mom and us kids stay behind. The new plan was to have us stay with family members throughout the summer to avoid the cost of renting. The remainder of that summer in Utah became one of the darkest periods of my life. Adjusting back to mainland living was difficult following our three years in paradise.

Our household of eight children, and essentially a single mother for the summer, put a lot of strain on my grandmother, so after staying with her for a few weeks we floated between other family members for another six weeks.

During that time, my older sister and I were invited to go to girls' camp with our cousins in Ogden. It had only been a few months since I attended girls' camp in Hawaii due to the difference in seasons.

Living in Utah was my first real experience living my religion "in the beehive," so to speak, and I found it to be quite different from my experiences outside of Utah. Overall it strengthened my convictions of what it meant to be, and not to be, a member of the LDS Church. I felt like members should be tightly knit and kind to one another.

Following camp, we returned to my cousins' house for a short time. When the pressure of caring for two families became too much for my aunt's, and still hoping for more time in Utah, my mom felt no choice but to find a rental. Then, deviating from the plan, we moved to West Valley. It was a change that caused a strain on our family finances. While living there my mom's health and ability to cope with the difficulties she was facing took a turn for the worse.

The rental was unfurnished, had no utilities, and was usually empty of food. We kids had to be creative to find things to do, and to find food to eat. Some neighbor kids who lived on a nearby farm knew we weren't eating properly and gave us vegetables from their garden.

For six weeks we slept on a bare floor in borrowed sleeping bags and only a few blankets and pillows, while mom went looking for more permanent housing, which was another deviation from the plan.

The stress of the situation began to take its toll on each of us. One thing led to another and by the end of the summer, dad had received word from a family member of how things had digressed. A few days before school started in New York, Dad drove across the country to pick us up.

I remember the tears on Dad's face when he learned of our living conditions and some of the things that had happened while we stayed behind in Utah.

That summer was a pivotal time in our family in general but also in my own life. I don't know all that happened, but I attribute the beginning of the decline of my parents' marriage to that three-month period.

As for my personal life, many dark and trying events I can't mention here took place, but I began to notice the double lives some men lived in Utah, including members of my distant family.

In my adulthood I've often looked back upon the events of that summer and have come to understand that many of my insecurities and natural defenses began during that time. In fact, some of what took place that summer seems to have been erased from my memory, which I believe is a natural result of unpleasant circumstances and young tender defense mechanisms. Discussing that summer brings me a great deal of discomfort when speaking or thinking about them today.

My fifth grade photo in Hawaii.

CHAPTER FIVE

---✦---

European Lessons

I was relieved to have my family reunited and grateful for the improved circumstances of our next home in Liverpool, a small bedroom community in Upstate New York. My father was attending school at Syracuse University, about a 30 minute drive away. Dad found a home to rent, since our stay would be so short.

Still, having just experienced a very difficult summer in Utah, and having gone from the tropical paradise of Hawaii only months before to the cold climate of New York, I found myself slipping into depression. Additionally, I was yet again facing a new school with new friends, at a time when girls' young emotions tend to become more complicated, and my parents had new struggles of their own.

Around that time we celebrated the birth of my second youngest sister, and my parents' ninth child. A short time later my thirteenth birthday was celebrated by a blizzard that brought depression and coldness along with its five foot snow drifts.

One of the advantages of living in Liverpool was living so close to Palmyra, a well-known historical location for Latter-day Saints, and a number of other popular church history sites such as the Smith Homestead, the Martin Harris home, and the Sacred Grove where Joseph Smith received his First Vision. Of all those places, I cherished the Sacred Grove most, and had my own sacred experiences there.

Visiting those historic sites, receiving promptings from the spirit, and my own pure desire led my maturing thirteen year old heart and mind to understand and gain a firm witness of what I had been taught throughout my life. With my dad working as Chaplain in the U.S. military, we frequently attended the sermons and meetings of other Christian denominations; sometimes attending up to five hours of services on Sundays between going to dad's "work church" and our LDS meetings. Those visits gave me something to compare to my experiences within my own faith.

For example, I always knew the Book of Mormon was true and was an inspired book, but the spirit placed a natural curiosity within me about the word keystone, and I became interested in what that meant, which led me to research. I read the Book of Mormon for the first time when I was 13. I read it within a few months and then sought answers and gained my own witness of Joseph Smith.

I gained my own testimony that Joseph Smith had in fact seen God the Father, and Jesus Christ his son in the Sacred Grove, and that he actually translated the Book of Mormon. All the while I was able to compare my thoughts and feelings with the experiences I had from visiting other faiths.

I felt a bond with Joseph Smith. As I've gained more experience with things of the light, I have noticed an increase in what I call "adversarial attacks," which are attempts of the adversary to stop my mission. I came to realize that Joseph knew full well what I've experienced in those dark encounters. When he went to that New York grove seeking the Lord in prayer in the spring of 1820, he recorded the following:

I had scarcely done so, when immediately I was seized upon by some power which entirely overcame me, and had such an astonishing influence over me as to bind my tongue so that I could not speak. Thick darkness gathered around me, and it seemed to me for a time as if I were doomed to sudden destruction.

But what immediately followed after that experience was undoubtedly one of the sweetest experiences of Joseph's life. I identified with his contrasting experiences of dark followed by light, and have felt that often in my life. My relatively short experience in New York was characterized by a deepened sense of spirituality and faith, and I was grateful for my time there.

Germany

In 1986, we flew from New York to Frankfurt, and then drove from there on to the military base in Heidelberg, Germany. We spent six weeks there in guest housing before finding a rental home in the little village of Baldsfeld, one hour from the base. We would end up spending over two and a half years in that spacious, eight-bedroom home.

Even though everyone spoke English on the base, I was required to take German in my 8th grade Middle School class, which was positioned on the base. During my first school year a new kid named Mike moved in only three weeks after school started, so all the girls were googily eyed over him. He was cocky, and I could tell he was a wild boy, but he really was the best looking guy in school. I liked him, but would never admit it to anyone. He flirted with me, but I constantly shot his advances at me down. He didn't like the rejection.

One day in gym class we were playing a game of dodge ball, when Mike's buddy "pantsed" me. It was humiliating! Then adding insult to injury, Mike took his turn a few minutes later, pantsing and humiliating me again! I was furious! But I had been given some foresight as to where he would be after he got changed in the locker room, and what I would do. I just didn't know how serious it would turn out.

I hurried and got changed and took my athletic bag containing my gym shoes and clothes and then waited for him to come out. Just as his face came into view I flung my bag at him, hitting him squarely in the nose as I said in tears, "Don't you ever do that to me again!"

He was shocked as all get out, and his buddies laughed at him for getting a bloody nose from a girl. The gym coach came out wondering what all the ruckus was about. I let him know I had been pantsed twice and that I was only defending myself.

Fortunately, I had developed a good reputation and the coach let me off the hook. It only made Mike like me more, but he never messed with me again. Despite trying to appear tough, knowing that I got Mike in trouble and that I humiliated him secretly broke my heart. I cried myself to sleep that night.

The following year I transitioned to Heidelberg American High School, which was also on the base. It was a tight knit community. While I was well behaved and respectful of my teachers, I was frequently sneaking in quiet conversations with my friends every chance I had. I have a lot of memories from that year in school. We were an athletic family, and my sport of choice was junior varsity volleyball. My siblings and I had friends on the base from the local village as well.

Communication with the kids was interesting, as the German kids spoke broken English, and we spoke broken German. That was where I developed my love for hazelnut spread as we swapped our American peanut butter for German Nutella with the local kids.

We had many travel and sight-seeing opportunities while living in Germany. I had the privilege of traveling to Paris for a weekend with friends. We went on a vacation to an Italian beach, where we camped for two weeks. We also went to Florence, Italy, and climbed the Tower of Pisa; and we traveled all over Germany and saw nearly all of the historic castles. We also went to the Swiss Alps, home of the famous Von Trapps, and saw the lands filmed in the classic musical *The Sound of Music.*

One of the more notable memories I have was traveling to East Berlin with my Dad in May of 1989, about six months before the wall came down. One of my dad's friends drove me, my dad, and my older sister in his car, acting as our escort and tour guide. We drove from Heidelberg passing several check points along the way; the most notable of which was Checkpoint Charlie. The men holding machine guns and the dramatic difference from one side of the border to the other left a deep impression on me.

The Mark exchange rate at the time was ten to one. That meant that our tight financial circumstances loosened up as my dad treated us to a fancy restaurant that included a seven-course meal. Coming from a large family, opportunities like that were rare. I remember my dad gave the waiter a $45 tip.

The first thing I noticed after passing into East Germany was the transition from first-world buildings and lifestyles to a more third-world, humble type of living based on survival rather than recreation and entertainment. Anything visible on the Communist side from the border of West Germany had a façade and the false appearance that East Germany was just like West Germany, but I knew it wasn't true. Through a spiritual lens I sensed a heightened level of darkness that began right at the border.

Watching the locals wait in lines for several hours to acquire their daily rations, and purchasing household commodities like food, clothing, or diapers created a searing image in my mind and heart. Very few families could afford a single car, and when they could, only the smallest cars were used. Most of the people going in to East Germany were not able to drive the areas we drove due to my dad's status in the military, which offered some measure of protection from being pulled over by local law enforcement. While in East Germany we did some sightseeing, and went to some museums.

My visionary gifts were a daily occurrence while living in Germany. It didn't matter where I was or what I was doing, I was frequently in vision. Germany and Europe's rich and colorful history came to life before me. I was shown in vision about the settling of the region by the Mongols centuries before, and the bloodshed and tumult that had gone on for a very long time.

One day we went to a large Russian cemetery, and I began to sense the presence of hundreds of disembodied spirits, many of which I understood had been killed during World War I and II, as well as numberless family members and ancestors of those who had fallen. There was a tangible sense of fear, lack of trust, and sorrow held among them. I knew of the Secret Service, and sensed something of their motives to get family members to turn on each other, create chaos, and cause heartache.

On another occasion there had been a beautiful snowfall in the village where we lived, so my siblings and I went outside for some sledding fun. As I took my turn downhill a vision became superimposed over my physical senses in the scene before me. I saw a depiction of a war that had taken place in that location at a time I would guess to be in the 1800s. It wasn't of men in proper military garb, but was more of a peasant uprising, based on their mode of dress.

Another very common occurrence of strong visionary experiences would take place as I frequently visited Germany's historic and beautiful castles, but to me they were only beautiful in their construction and in the way they had been cared for and preserved in modern times. I loved the perfectly trimmed gardens, and well-manicured lawns and shrubbery. The artwork was breathtaking and struck a deep chord in my soul, as art often does for me. But what was invisible to most people on the insides of those magnificent structures in times past was far from beautiful.

Of all the castles, my family went to the Heidelberg Castle most often because that was near our high school and the army base where we lived. It was also where I attended the Junior Prom. Other notable structures we visited were the Neuschwanstein, Hohenzollern, and Wartburg castles.

As I toured those castles with family, friends, or with school classes, I typically found myself among a company of other tourists listening to a tour guide provide a historical sketch of the kings that had lived there, and other various details. As those descriptions commenced I sensed in real-time the very things they described. Often as they began to describe the king's appearance, he would vividly appear before me through my spiritual eyes as if literally standing in front of me.

As the tours continued through the King's personal chambers, I would immediately sense the adulterous and illicit relationships that took place in those rooms. I saw kings beheading their wives over jealousies, and having sexual relations with their daughters and servants, with no regard for gender or social circumstance. I sensed the expression "off with her head" regularly in those places, as those kings in the heat of their passion proclaimed their final judgment upon their often innocent victims. In those halls I discerned numerous disembodied souls just hanging around, as if they had nowhere to go.

On one occasion my two year old sister began crying during an intense emotional moment. Things were so evil I had to leave, and told my mom I would take my sister out. In hindsight, I think my little sister, though only two, was disturbed for the same reasons I was. After having seen a number of those castles,

I reached a point that I no longer wanted to go in and would just wait in the car. Two or three castles in particular radiated such dark energy I refused to ever set foot in them.

While each castle had its own unique and vile historic makeup, common themes existed in all of them, with lust being at the top of the list. Lustful acts and sensations were strong in those corridors, along with sensations of insanity, carnal sensuality, murder, and conspiring oaths; dark passages, tunnels, hidden doorways, and torture chambers with their blood stains on the ground in token of their vile cruelties; rapes and torture of innocent women and children, and demonic possessions.

Those impressions and visual experiences caused me to ask the Lord what purpose He had in seeing and having me experiencing those things. Often in those moments of heightened emotions I would say in my heart, "Lord, why is this happening to me?" while I would want to hurry from the room or the castle to find fresh air and a chance to regroup and settle down.

Through those experiences, and particularly the intense feelings of lust that pervaded those walls, my ability to discern lust energy became extremely heightened. That keen sense would come to play an important role in my courting years later on, and would allow me to more easily recognize harmful and threatening situations, largely in part to what I experienced in those castles.

But as I had learned well by that time, the manifestations I was privileged and burdened to experience were mine alone, and as much as I wanted to speak about them with loved ones, I had no audience. I knew sharing those things with others would only lead to heartache, so I kept them to myself.

We were privileged on another trip to stand on the same ground, and set foot in some of the same buildings as the famous Von Trapp family. While in the beautiful Swiss Alps I was shown a reenactment of the soldiers who came in pursuit of the Von

Trapps following their concert as they hid from their would-be captors. The clarity of that experience was so acute that I saw the faces and precise locations of where each person stood as they waited for their enemies to pass by. I saw the look of terror that overcame their mother as she held her hand to her child's mouth. The trepidation and fear that had been felt one hundred years before still hung in the air as if I had been there in person.

It was my pleasure and burden to visit "Eagles' Nest," Adolf Hitler's notorious and historically significant mountain getaway in the Bavarian Alps near the Austrian border. It was my pleasure because of the beautiful and historic setting; and my burden because I was shown some of the life of Hitler, including his raping of women and children, and his suicide. The thought of that man makes me physically ill.

While in Italy, I witnessed firsthand the nature of open European sexuality, immodesty, and European men's impure affection practices. One time I was floating down the Rhine River with friends in a raft for a church activity. My friends and I were told if we got ahead of the main group to pull over and wait for the others to catch up, which we ended up doing. When we pulled over, we found that we had stopped at a nude beach and to our innocent surprise we beheld a tanned and wrinkly German man in his seventies shouting, "Hallow Americanas, hallow, come and see here." It was the first time I had ever seen a naked man.

On the same float trip, we needed to stop again, and my friends got off the raft and went to explore. I had been given a quick visual of what lie ahead for my friends and said, "I don't think we should go over there." They didn't listen to me, so I waited behind. After a couple minutes they came back screaming as they had come upon a few teenagers engaged in inappropriate and immodest activities.

On a trip to Italy, a friend and my younger brother and I were walking along the edge of the beach in our swimsuits, with me walking closest to the water. Just ahead were about fifteen men spanning the ages of 15 to 20, standing near the water holding buckets. Six or seven older men were lying on their stomachs at the edge of the water with their arms outstretched.

As we drew closer to them, the young men began charging toward us as if they were going to playfully throw buckets of water on us. As we passed by the older men grabbed hold of our ankles. Before I knew it, they pulled me and my friend into the water as they ripped at our swimsuits and groped us. My brave younger brother called them out on their perversion and yelled at them to stop. After lots of kicking and screaming, they left us alone.

I had a similar experience in the Tower of Pisa. When my family and I climbed the narrow staircases on our way toward the top, a number of unfriendly European men coming from the other direction forcefully and inappropriately groped at me. I felt violated and disgusted by their lust and lack of self-control.

Those and dozens of similar experiences seared into my soul the illicit tendencies of men who objectify and sexually demean women. You could say that I am hypersensitive to inappropriate sexual energy, whether from thoughts, words, or actions, and I can pick men like this out of a crowd. I have absolutely no tolerance for lustful behavior and find it sad that there are so many who struggle with this.

After serving as a bishop for the LDS church, my dad was called as the new Stake President of the Stuttgart, Germany Stake. He would leave for work at 5:00 a.m., and get home late several days a week, and then his ecclesiastical responsibilities took him away for the weekends. I don't feel like I saw much of my dad during our three years in Germany, due to his church callings and job. He worked hard and I missed him.

During my sophomore year of high school, my family won

the Great American Family Award of the year. That bestowal of recognition led to our guest appearance on a news station as we were broadcast on military bases all over Europe and in newspapers as well. I was teased relentlessly at school for it. Coming from a big family brought jokes from guys at school who had crude humor and that award brought jealousy from others.

I knew our family had weaknesses along with some strengths, so the accolade came with mixed emotion. As my mom spoke on the air and touted some of our accomplishments, I heard the words "Pride cometh before the fall" three times. I began to develop the sense that my family would come apart at the seams in the future, not quite understanding how that might happen. I had the sense that we were headed for some rough days ahead, but I had no idea how bad it would get. In another five years, I would see my impression fulfilled.

Common stake functions for Latter-day Saints at the stake level included stake dances and youth conferences. Those events required a lot of planning and coordination, especially when factoring in so many people from a diversity of countries and cultures. My favorite part of the conferences was testimony meeting, an event where the youth get a turn to speak before their peers and share their feelings about God, faith, and their religion.

I loved those meetings for the tender feelings they brought, and was especially touched to see some of the young men get emotional when speaking about God. It was a test in a way for me to determine those boys who had real substance.

Youth conferences were designed to provide spiritual experiences for young adults, but there were other valuable lessons I learned from them as well. One night in Stuttgart after attending testimony meeting and the lights had all gone out; some boys from another building snuck out and came to the window of our room. They tried to get us to sneak out. I sensed a visitor from the other side come in to our room. As I considered going with my roommates to meet the boys, I distinctly felt a firm hand on my shoulder and heard a voice say "Stay!"

I went to bed as my two roommates left through the window. The next day I found out there had been some kissing, and the boys had regrettably gotten a little carried away with their hands. My friends regretted their decisions and I felt sorry for them, but was grateful I had listened to my visitor.

The dances and other activities occurred on about a monthly basis, and were a lot of fun. I learned they would always be the most fun when the Munich and K-town boys came. I had been taught that it wasn't polite to refuse a boy's request to dance. That combined with the fact I always tried to be kind to everyone, I found that all types of boys were attracted to me, some of which put me in awkward social situations. I often felt trapped in some of those conditions, but in hindsight I was glad I experienced what I did and for the lessons I learned.

Moving back to the states created yet another emotional experience. That move was initiated by a new promotion my dad had received as Lt. Colonel, and his next station was at the Pentagon in Washington D.C. We purchased a home in Northern Virginia, where the cost of living was very high, and for several weeks we had no furniture in our home. We moved in August between my sophomore and junior years of school. I remember going through a period of depression over the transition. I loved my time in Germany, and missed it a great deal!

With a family of twelve it became increasingly important for everyone in the family to contribute, so we took on some paper routes in order to supplement our income. As my dad went into D.C. each morning, my mom and six younger siblings went in one of our station wagons and completed paper-routes. My younger brother and I took a route in the other station wagon.

We had early morning seminary, so I had to wake up at 4:15 a.m. to complete the paper route by 5:30 a.m. I would then go home and get ready for school and seminary which began at 6:00 a.m.

After a year and a half of delivering papers, on a dark morning, I took one side of the road as my brother took the other, just as we had always done. We entered a cul-de-sac and as I lost view of my brother, my senses became heightened and I anticipated that a man would jump from behind a bush, and I had a full understanding of the man's impure intentions. Along with my foresight of the man came an understanding of where to run to effectively get away from him and find safety. I sensed a guardian angel nearby adding an additional measure of protection.

Moments later, a man in his thirties jumped out from the bush just as I had seen. He got close enough that I could sense his breath just behind me as I took off running in the direction I had been shown previously, and made it safely to the car. My brother had also been given a prompting to run for the car and reached it at the same time. I knew by the grace of God I had avoided catastrophe. For several months I had been asking my parents to quit the paper route, so when I told my parents what happened, they gave me permission to quit. I finished out the week and moved on to other things.

At the end of my Senior year, my after school responsibilities took their toll on my social life. My junior year I put away the student government activities that I had been so involved in during previous school years. I loved volleyball, but it wasn't part of the athletic program at my school in Virginia.

I began taking an interest in doing things that would help others and benefit society. I volunteered at the city fire department, at a local home for mentally handicapped children once a week, visited the elderly in nursing homes, and worked as a volunteer for Rape Crisis in the community. It was nice to be able help others. In addition to the humanitarian activities I picked up a job as a dental assistant for two years during my junior and senior years.

It was a privilege to have my grandma Hanchett living with us in Virginia. I didn't have a lot of friends, and my Gram became a trusted friend. We would talk for hours. She was the only one I felt I could share my dreams and visions with, because Gram had dreams of her own. She had some prophetic dreams that came true involving her children and grandchildren. She had dreams of the Tree of Life like me, and also had some dreams concerning the Second Coming of the Savior.

The summer before my junior year of high school, I developed a great friendship with a young man named Eric. We had a strong spiritual connection and often had deep and meaningful conversations.

He and I dated for about two months, until Eric graduated and went to a semester at BYU. He came home for Christmas at the semester break, and then prepared to go on his mission in January. I liked him a lot, and was drawn to his genuine nature, loving heart, his love of the Lord and his great example of kindness and deep spiritual conviction. I often wondered if he was to be my husband. The night before he was set apart as a missionary we had a tender conversation and shared a single kiss. He gave me a CTR ring in hope of keeping our relationship going for the next two years.

One week following Eric's departure, I began to experience some peculiar dreams related to my future husband. With the timing of Eric leaving I couldn't help wondering if it meant that I had found my husband. One of those dreams became recurring for years to come. It took several years until I had enough clarity to understand what it meant. It was a dream of my future husband. This is how the dream went:

I was standing over the edge of a valley, holding a baby in my left arm that looked to be about six months old. I thought the baby was a boy, but wasn't quite sure. To my right was a little boy with light brown hair who looked to be about three years old. To the left of the boy stood a man who I knew was my husband. He was tall, dark, and handsome, but had a blurred face. I knew he stood over six feet tall, but couldn't tell just how tall he was. The dream always ended the same. Just as I was about to see his face, we would turn from the valley scene before us to go back to our car.

I could see the faces of the children, but never saw my husband's face. I could feel his energy and sensed his warm smile. I probably had that dream once a month for the next seven years, often waking up in tears, frustrated from getting so close to seeing his face, but never seeing his eyes. He was truly the mystery man of my dreams.

I kept writing Eric for the next eighteen months, not really knowing if he was the man in my dreams. He always signed his letters back to me, "Your friend, Eric," trying to be a valiant and faithful missionary. When time came for me to move to Provo, my parents arranged for my friend and her parents to drive me there.

Graduation from West Springfield High School
in Springfield, Virginia in 1991.

CHAPTER SIX

❧

College Commotion

As college drew nearer I was excited and nervous to be out on my own. I was looking forward to a new social life and to advancing my education. Academic life came naturally. Despite the new academic and social possibilities that came with student life, school wasn't all fun. I didn't have a car, which complicated getting a job, so my main mode of transportation my freshman year was on foot. During my sophomore year I used roller blades, and for my junior year I used a bike.

My financial situation wasn't ideal. I didn't have a job during my first semester as I settled into the college scene. I had worked and saved money for tuition and housing in the dorms, and I'd paid that before arriving at BYU so that was covered, but I had very little left over that I brought with me.

I brought enough money to pay for a semester of eating in the dorm cafeteria, and the rest I had left in my bank account with the understanding that my mom was going to send me the rest once I got to Provo. I had a joint bank account at the Credit Union with my parents, and my mom promised to send me my money once I got settled into school.

October came, but no money had been sent. I called my mom asking for her to please send me my money. She fedexed a

$25 check. I waited a few more weeks. Still no money from my mom. I did my best to stretch the money, since I didn't have a credit or debit card to be able to access the funds I had saved. I called again. Finally in early December another $25 check arrived. To this day I'm not quite sure how I got by financially that first year of college.

I put a high priority on my social life during school. I was particularly eager to resolve the mystery of the unknown face in my dreams that would one day become my husband. I often found myself scanning crowds at sporting events and other social gatherings, scanning the men in church meetings, or visiting temple grounds in hope of finding inspiration from within the building I could not yet enter. I was constantly trying to find a man whose energy and appearance best matched the man in my dream.

Out of sensitivity to my husband and those I dated who are married to others, I'm not going to share my experiences with relationships of those I considered marrying. I had many positive and uplifting experiences, but I also went through some heart-wrenching experiences. I have chosen to share just a few that taught me more about my gifts and that left strong impressions on my tender heart. I learned great lessons and came to understand more about the atonement because of these experiences.

I was frequently dating, but never got serious with anyone during my freshman year. Overall I had a lot of good guy friends. On a normal week I would have five to ten casual dates. Because of the strong impressions and visuals of my recurring dream, I tried to focus on dating men over six feet tall, and who had dark brown hair.

Whenever I began to see that one of my boyfriends didn't quite match my dream I would end the relationship, usually after a few weeks, but some lasted several months. I mention only a few of those relationships here because of the effect they had on my heart and the lessons I learned from them.

My roommates were eager to help me find my mystery man. One night during my first semester in 1991, there was a floor date among the dorm residents that I didn't want to attend. In a last ditch effort to drag me along, my roommates asked me to describe the kind of guy that could provide some incentive for me to go. I described the man in my dream to them as being over six feet tall, any color of eyes (since I didn't know his eye color), and dark brown hair. They looked through the dorm photo book and found three matches.

One of them was Alex, but he had a girlfriend. Another match was a guy who messed around with girls and I wasn't interested in that; and the last match was a guy named Jeff Rowe. I was told by my friends that Jeff already had a date, so I decided I wouldn't go. Unbeknownst to me, Jeff did not have a date that night. In fact Jeff knew nothing of the floor date. He had not been asked to go on the floor date, but I didn't know that until editing this book.

During my first semester I met a 19-year-old guy named Will, who was from California. His parents owned and operated an asbestos removal company. He was one of my closest guy friends during my freshman year. We never officially dated, but were just really good friends. One day he told me, "Julie, you're a really good girl. I don't think I deserve a girl like you."

This made me sad. I liked Will. He was a nice guy. Lots of fun and always very kind to me. He didn't think he was good enough for me. He asked if I would ever give a guy like him a chance. He had made some mistakes in high school, but he had repented.

He hoped that after his mission we could date. I told him I believed in the atonement and if I was still single when he came home from his mission I would date him. He ended up going on a mission. We didn't write while he was on his mission, but reconnected when he got home and we became good friends again my junior year.

Before long I became interested in a guy named Jeff. He was athletic and fit the profile of the man in my dream well, but that relationship didn't last long. I wasn't as spiritually connected to Jeff as I had been with Eric from high school, but there was a strong physical attraction. Eric became my standard for friendship and spiritual attraction.

Some of the guys I dated were in the same financial situation I was in, so we learned to have inexpensive fun. Those often turned out to be the best dates; one of which was a double date with some friends and a guy I didn't know well. We went sledding at Sundance Ski Resort north of Provo, which I later found out was illegal, or I wouldn't have gone.

As we sledded toward the bottom of the hill, we were headed right for a large metal pipe. Just then we hit a mogul, which caused the sled to flip, and the next thing I knew we were all laying on the ground. Interestingly, I was thirty feet from the sled and my date. I was later shown in vision that I had heavenly help that day, and was picked up and moved, which caused me to avoid a dangerous situation, aside from some damage to my neck and back. I remember the following week someone went down the same slope and broke their back.

My first year of school was largely characterized as getting settled into the college routine, finding my place socially, and learning more about myself. When summer break of 1992 came, I went home to live with my parents for three weeks. My dad was then reassigned three hours north to Pennsylvania where he would attend War College. For the remainder of the summer I stayed in Virginia living with a friend, while I worked as a dental office manager. A couple of my brothers also stayed back to work, and we would drive to our parent's home together in

Pennsylvania on the weekends. As that summer rolled on I went home less and less, as my parent's marriage was failing and it became too much for me to witness firsthand.

The spring before my sophomore year, my parents bought a Condominium at Enclave in Provo. Since I would be living in the condo, and so that we could qualify for owner occupied financing. My parents put the deed in my name and my dad's name.

My older sister who managed the condo for the first semester was graduating and moving to Kansas with her husband for graduate school. I resumed the responsibility for managing the condo, collecting rent and making sure things ran smoothly. As a fairly upper class residence at the time, I often felt like a misfit among the other girls, many of which came from wealthy families. I didn't have a lot of money and was responsible for supporting myself.

I loved the outdoor recreation opportunities of Utah. One of my favorite things to do was hiking at Bridal Veil Falls in Provo Canyon, and Kiwanis Park. I biked or roller-bladed to and from my job, school, and 15 miles to the gym where I worked out six days a week. With all the physical exertion I had gotten in the best shape I had ever been in physically. Before long I was leg squatting 350 lbs, one time maxing out at 550 lbs, and bench pressing 150 lbs.

At the age of 20, I was hired full-time as the office manager of a portfolio management firm. I worked there for about three years until I got married. In addition to managing the office, I was able to go on the occasional business conference attending Investment Seminars, called "ISI's", seeking clients with net worth's of $1 Million or more. Those conferences were great for professional networking and business skills, which would provide needed experience and skills later in my life with regard to my mission.

I also learned a bit of the darker side of the business world. It was common to try to draw potential clients into vendor booths by luring them in with a young and attractive young woman. While at those conferences I frequently turned down other vendors' bribes to have me switch companies and help them front their booths.

Fronting their booths wasn't always all they wanted. On a Las Vegas trip a total stranger offered me $1,000 to sleep with him. On other occasions, in exchange for a single night rendezvous I was offered a Rollex, a trip to California, or $11,000 from a guy in the casino; all of which I turned down for my $7.50 an hour job.

The contrast between my professional life by day and my student life at night was stark. During the day I was dealing with the constant and unsought come-on's by wealthy men of the business world, and would then go back to my student life.

I soon began thinking more about Eric, my high school friend who I knew would be returning from his mission soon. As I thought of him and knew he still had several months to complete, I heard a distinct voice saying, "Eric is not your husband. You need to stop writing him." I was obedient to the message I received and never wrote him another letter, even though I received one more letter from him.

The next semester, shortly after my 19th birthday, Eric came home from his mission. He hadn't been home long before he went to my parents' home in Pennsylvania, to ask for my phone number. He called me in Utah and we had a seven hour phone conversation. I told him everything that had happened in my life, got emotional, and really opened up to him about some of my challenges. During that call he professed his love for me and told me that he had no intention of dating anyone else.

His family was moving from Virginia to Utah a few months later, the week after school got out. He asked me if we could get together when he came out west. By that time, I had learned a little more about the dark haired but still faceless husband of my dreams. I had also been given several visuals of a blond hair, blue eyed woman in Eric's future. I had been warned not to mention my visionary insights concerning others but I felt compelled by the spirit to encourage him to begin dating other people. My heart broke as I did so and I cried to him on the phone.

While I still liked Eric, the message I had received was clear: "Eric is not your husband." When winter semester ended in April, Eric's family moved west only five days later as planned. I made sure to leave Utah for Virginia just before he arrived. Seeing him would have been too hard on my already hurting heart.

That summer Eric started dating the blond-hair blue-eyed girl that would eventually become his wife. In September of 1992 we went out one time, and for the next three weeks he attempted to reconnect with me. One time as I was walking up a hill on campus, he approached me and I started to run from him as he shouted out, "Julie, wait! Please wait!"

It broke my heart! He never knew how much I loved him, and despite the anguish of my soul, I knew he wasn't the one for me. That was the last time I saw him single. In upcoming years I would observe Eric dating, marrying, and having children, all while I remained single. Each occurrence served a measure of salt to my emotional wounds caused from our breakup.

That fall semester in 1992 I hung out with an apartment full of guys, with good values and who were a lot of fun. Things began to get serious with a guy named Brad from Payson, Utah, who was a close fit to the husband in my dream, which kept recurring and I couldn't leave it alone. I earnestly tried to find direction and guidance concerning the men I dated.

I read my patriarchal blessing weekly, prayed daily, dated often, read and studied the scriptures, and wrote in my journal faithfully. I knew how to receive personal revelation and knew the Lord was guiding me in the decision to break up with Brad after about three months of dating. We broke things off, causing both of us broken hearts, but we still saw each other often.

Each of the men I dated left an impression upon me. The price of having a big heart was steep, as each breakup caused heartache which often felt like more than I could bear. But knowing my heart, the Lord continued to guide me and heal my heart. I knew He loved me and knew He had a very specific plan for me. I wanted to follow that plan.

My breakup with Brad seemed to be the beginning point of a dark chapter in my life. Over the next year I would experience and be witness to some really unusual things; some of which most people never experience in a lifetime. As a visiting teaching coordinator, I worked closely with the Relief Society presidency, which helped me get to know the girls in my ward fairly well. It also gave me inside knowledge to some of the events that were going on. That year, eight girls in my condo complex became pregnant; half of which were attending BYU, and the other half were students at UVSC.

During Christmas break my roommate sold her contract to a girl named Tina who had moved in from Chicago. Due to the change in management with my sister leaving, Tina didn't have a proper background check. If she had been checked properly they would have found that she was a con-artist and had records in eleven different states for credit card fraud. She was a suspect for other crimes.

For three months Tina had been writing a large number of fraudulent checks to me as her landlord for utilities and rent. Within a short time she owed me $3,300. At the end of the day the responsibility for paying the mortgage on the condo fell on my shoulders, so if the tenants didn't pay up, it came out of my already very shallow pockets. Having gotten to know Tina on a personal level, my gifts provided clarity concerning things about her life. I discerned that she had mental illness and was a pathological liar.

In February one of my roommates reported Tina to the Police. Local law enforcement got involved to work with my roommates in planning and performing a sting operation to try to keep her from leaving town in order to bring her into compliance with the law. Two weeks later on a Sunday my roommates invited a number of friends from the complex over to help load Tina's moving truck, and provided dinner to anyone who would help. Tina's plan was to move to Oregon the next day, or so that was her story; I had discerned that she was actually planning on going to California.

She needed some packing tape and groceries for her trip the next day. My roommates and I went along with the plan to support the investigators behind the operation. We drove her moving truck to the Food for Less in Orem, which has since been demolished. While there, I recognized a 6'4", 220 pound grocery checker, who I had often seen at the gym where I worked out. I had also seen him in vision.

When I glanced at him, I noticed he was looking me up and down. He was very good looking, but I was repulsed by his energy and even felt a little afraid of him. I noticed that he recognized my fear which further excited him, so I decided it would be best to get out of the store.

I told my roommates, Lisa and Emily, "I'm going to go get the moving truck and meet you guys up front", which I did. As they climbed into the truck I sensed their giddy and eager excitement about something. They knew that I had just broken up with Brad and wanted to do me a favor. So, they provided the grocery store checker, Nick, with our address and encouraged him to come to dinner at 6 p.m. I was nervous.

Brad showed up for dinner and to help load Tina's truck. He

told me of his hope to keep our relationship going, right around the time Nick showed up. Nick astutely picked up on the break up that was in progress, and the feelings I still had for Brad.

As we loaded the truck, each time Nick found me alone he took the chance to hit on me saying things like, "So what's with this Brad guy? You know you want me." Despite his unruly boldness, he was strangely charming. Still, I had just met him and so I responded to his arrogance saying, "Who do you think you are? I don't even know you!"

He then said in his most charismatic voice, "Doesn't matter. You know you want me." I would go and grab another box and when I returned I was met with more of the same: "You know you want me." His cocky seduction continued throughout the night.

The next day as Tina pulled away in her moving truck she was stopped by the police and eventually indicted. I didn't play a significant role in it, but the sting operation had been successful. Tina called me a short time later and harassed me for having any involvement, even thought she still owed me $3,300. The last I heard of her, she ended up getting married and moving to Japan.

Following the night at Food for Less, Nick came to the condo every day. I was conflicted. I had just ended a relationship, was struggling to meet my mortgage payment thanks to Tina, and to top it off I had just received word that my parents were separating.

I was in no condition for starting a romance, but Nick was interesting. He was very aggressive, but he was charming, and he did show interest, which during my time of confusion was comforting, so I didn't mind him visiting me as a friend.

After three weeks of hanging out with Nick, his demeanor began to take on a more assertive, less charming side. His former comments, "You know you want me" turned into "If I can't have you, no one can." Looking back I can see that he had a subtle and persistent way of working my defenses down to his aggressiveness, all during a time of conflict.

A few weeks later as winter semester drew to a close, Nick had a plan to pick up a new SUV in his home town of Stockton, California. He wanted someone to go along for the drive with him back to Utah. He asked me to go with him. I had never been to Sacramento and thought it could be fun; and a vacation from my troubles sounded great.

One of Nick's friends drove me and Nick to the Salt Lake City airport. As we were waiting to board, I recalled the spirit clearly telling me three times, "Don't go!"

In my depressed, emotionally raw, and vulnerable state of mind, I thought to myself, "I don't care. I'm going anyway." Then we boarded the plane for Sacramento.

After Nick and I did some sightseeing and he took me around his hometown for two days, Nick's mother pulled me aside in the bathroom and said, "Honey, I don't know how well you know Nick. You seem like such a nice girl. Nick has a chemical imbalance and drug problems, and I'm not sure why you're with him."

She further explained that he was sent home early from his mission on a medical discharge due to his imbalance. She explained that he had a lot of problems, and felt like I deserved better than Nick.

The next day Nick bought the SUV he had his eye on and we made plans to head back to Utah. As we began to leave I heard three times, "Don't get in that car."

I disregarded my prompting and got in anyway. After we had been in the car for a few hours we stopped in Reno Nevada. Nick fueled up and went into the store and bought some CDs. It disappointed me because it was a Sunday, which I let him know. He didn't seem to care too much.

Shortly after leaving Reno on a long and isolated stretch of highway, I received a visual of a scene that caught me off guard. I begged and pleaded with God that what I was seeing was only a figment of my imagination and would not come to pass. I then heard the words "We love you Julie. We love you."

Just then I saw my Grandpa Hanchett. It was a tender but somber moment for me, as I began to feel the gravity of the situation I found myself in.

Nick pulled to the side of the road. He spoke in an aggressive voice demanding that I do certain things to him, which I adamantly refused to do. He grabbed me and violently threw me in the back seat. I began screaming "Please stop!!" as he cackled and said, "You think you're so good? You're such a prude; you think you're too good for me?"

His verbal abuse and laughing continued as he sexually assaulted me. I continued begging, shouting, and attempting to free myself, but I was powerless against him. Then, just as had happened to me on the operating table as a child, my spirit began to detach from my body in what felt like a divine sort of protective measure.

For the next two hours I sat in silent bewilderment as we drove back to Provo—defiled, abused, demeaned, and completely violated as he laughed at and continued to mock me. When we arrived in Provo, he stopped at Food for Less, making me sit in the front seat of his new car, waiting for him so he could pick up his paycheck. He dropped me to the curb at my condo and pulled away.

My disgust and fear for Nick reached new levels as he continued to come to my condo. I didn't let anyone know what had happened to me, fearing for my life; the shame and guilt consuming me. I was constantly telling my roommates to close the door and keep it locked. I spread the word of my fear of Nick to all the guys in the complex, and even developed a code system with them using telephones, just in case anything were to happen. One ring and a hang up meant I was in trouble and that help was needed. I also informed my church leaders that Nick was stalking me.

The system didn't work. My roommates still left me alone and often left the front door wide open. Nick would watch the condo closely and knew when everyone was gone but me. On one occasion he barged right through the front door in a fit of rage. He came upstairs and into my room, where I was reading my scriptures. He pushed me against the wall and said, "You think you're so good, you prude! If I can't have you no one can, do you hear me? I will kill you!"

He threatened to kill me if I told anyone what he had done. I did everything I could to get help. I even called 911 to let them know I was being stalked, and of the abuse I was receiving, but they effectively told me there really wasn't much they could do until he attacked me again.

For another three months over the summer break Nick continued to harass me, but his intensity and peculiar interest in me miraculously tapered off. Nick moved back home to California the following October, and I never saw him in life again. For years to come I lived in daily fear that he would find me.

In the weeks and months that followed I often asked the Lord why he allowed me to be assaulted. Through vision and dreams I was given a number of hypothetical scenarios of how it might have turned out, and I gained a sense of how much protection I had actually been given, and how it could have been much worse. I learned that Nick's abuse, and many other men who made evil sexual attempts on me were essentially used as pawns by the adversary.

I considered filing a formal complaint against Nick with the city police and BYU, but with his threats on my life, I couldn't bring myself to do it. I was a classic case of a number of sexual abuse victims over the years at BYU who have lived in too much fear of their stalkers and predators to report them. I lived with the fear of the repercussions and judgment that would surely follow from others.

Things in my family life had declined significantly by that time. I didn't take news of my parents upcoming divorce well. For two days I lay in bed, unable to function, having lost my appetite. My roommates stopped me from removing all my family photos down from the bulletin board and from ripping up my scrapbooks. I recalled the impression I had from my sophomore year in high school back in Germany, "Pride cometh before the fall," as "the fall" I had been warned of was being played out before my eyes.

The events that had taken place in my life in less than a year caused very deep anguish, emotionally, physically, and spiritually. But I was blessed to have a bishop who helped me through the difficult time. Interestingly, that bishop served for only eight months, beginning in February of that year when I first met Nick, and lasting until the month Nick moved from Utah. That bishop helped navigate me through my con-artist roommate experience, my parents' divorce, and my experience with Nick, among other things. His release came about so he could begin working in the Missionary Training Center.

Before leaving as my bishop, he had begun helping me work through the process of applying to the church missionary program; something I considered for years. My bishop and I would connect as missionaries at the MTC a few months later. His coming and going during the most difficult chapter of my life was too coincidental to be coincidence.

It was the type of occurrence that has helped convince me that there really are no coincidences in life, but that there are divine orchestrations by a loving Father in Heaven. I felt like my bishop was put there just for me.

After I had worked through many of the challenges of that school year, my friend Chris came home from his mission. We went on a date to get reacquainted and I was eager to learn if he was the man from my dream. I found that I still loved his heart and good nature, and we had a spiritual connection but the chemistry was missing. I also knew of the feelings he still had for his high school girlfriend. As we were sitting on my couch I very clearly heard the words "Chris is not your husband." The conflict from my impression and the deep friendship we had was heart wrenching, and caused me some tears that night. The last I heard of Chris he had married his high school sweetheart, and lived in Michigan with four children.

A short time later my good friend Will from freshman year also came back from his mission. We kept running into each other at the most random times and places, so we reconnected our friendship where it had left off two years previously. I was grateful to have a good guy friend who I could trust and who wasn't interested in starting a romance.

Our relationship had an interesting dynamic. He would hang out with his girlfriend who was attending Salt Lake Community College on weekends, and I was going out with other guys on weekends, but during the week we would hang out as friends. He was supportive of me during challenging times, and he would tell me about courting his girlfriend. Because we were so open about our relationships, we both just figured we didn't like each other in that way.

We would go to Hogi Yogi, and he always offered to pay, but I rarely took him up on it. He sometimes brought friends, which let me know that he really was just a friend and didn't want more than that. He never put any moves on me, except once when he held my hand during a movie. Several months went by and there were no other attempts at any form of affection. But I began to notice little red flags with Will that firmed up my confidence that he wasn't the guy in my dream.

As the semester rolled on, I had a number of bizarre encounters with men that confirmed to me that I had somehow been marked by the adversary as a target for sexual abuse. Sometime after I reconnected with Will, I developed another stalker, strikingly similar to my experience with Nick. He was also given my address by my roommates, worked out at the same gym, and also had blond hair and blue eyes, like Nick.

One night he showed up at my apartment as I was reading scriptures and he said, "Hey, you wanna make out?" I recognized him from the gym, but didn't know his name. I told him, "No. I don't." As my roommates left the apartment, I told him he needed to leave three times, and was met with resistance each time. I went to the front door and said, "Get out. Now!" When he realized his pitiful efforts for affection wouldn't be realized, he stepped out on the front porch, unzipped his pants and exposed himself for several seconds before stomping off.

On the day my parent's divorce was finalized, I ran into a guy named Craig that I had dated the year before. We had only hung out a few times, but fell out of touch. I had changed my address and gone unlisted following my experience with Nick.

Craig flagged me down when he saw me, and said he had been looking for me for nearly a year. I could tell he was still interested in me, but knew from the year prior that he didn't fit the man in my dream, so I wasn't eager to talk to him. We spoke for a moment and I agreed to meet him in a park. When we met, I cried and told him about my parents' divorce. He asked if we could start a relationship, and I let him know some of the things going on in my life at the time and that I wasn't ready for a relationship. After some persistence on his part, I settled on being friends, if he agreed to set firm boundaries with no physical affection.

For weeks he came over every day and honored my wishes.

There was no hand holding or kissing, just hanging out and good genuine fun. He was a tender, kind-hearted gentleman—more so than anyone I had known up to that time. After a few weeks I began to have visuals of some dark things surrounding his life. They were so dark, and they strongly contrasted the gentleman I had come to know, that I kept brushing them aside as figments of my imagination, and didn't believe they were possible.

I began to sense that he was living a double life and was heavily addicted to pornography, which at that time was most commonly available in magazines rather than the internet. I had a sense that he had been sleeping with other women. Still, he gave me no cause to believe that he was anything other than a gentleman.

I made the emotional conflict a serious matter of prayer, visiting the temple for three weeks, and sincerely seeking answers about the visuals I was having. The spirit's messages became increasingly clear, evolving from "Julie, you need to distance yourself from Craig," to "Julie, you need to get away now!" which eventually turned into, "Julie, Run!"

I took the messages seriously and began telling Craig we needed to part ways, but to no avail. I didn't want to hurt him, and couldn't bring myself to let him know why I was letting him go. And besides, I had no evidence for my suspicions. All I had was the spirit, my gifts, and the sheer faith that what I was seeing was true. In May I told him I could no longer see him.

It was a July night when I had a visual of being in Craig's house and viewing a stash of dirty magazines in his room, and catching him in the act of fornication. The very next day while riding my bike, I bumped into a guy I barely knew named Chris, who was the landlord for the home Craig was living in. He knew I had been seeing Craig and said to me "Julie, can you come to the house? I've got something to show you."

We went to Craig's house, and the dream I had the night

before played out as Chris showed me Craig's secret stash in the desk drawer. It was the physical proof I needed that Craig was living a double life. Chris then stood at a certain location and said in effect, "This is where I was standing when I saw Craig in the act of fornication." He then described the exact woman I had seen with Craig in vision.

Chris then asked me if I would like to catch him red-handed. Wanting some closure and validation of my visionary experiences I said yes. He called me a week later and said, "All right, there's a blonde-hair blue-eyed girl here right now, come on over." I pulled up to his house and parked across the street and found a red Ferrari parked in front of his house. I was given a preview of what he would be wearing, the expression on his face when I caught him, how he would act, and what I needed to say beforehand.

Craig lived in the basement of the home. It was a dark night and the lights on his front porch had burned out, which created optimal conditions for looking into the well-lit home; it didn't take much effort to see him through the window of the door. Chris knocked on the door at just the right moment, and yelled out, "Craig, Julie's here."

Craig jumped up and dressed himself quickly, as he closed the door to the bedroom and scrambled to the front door. I watched the expression of sheer horror on his face knowing he had been caught. It was difficult to believe that three weeks previously Craig had professed his love to me along with his interest in getting married.

For fifteen minutes we spoke on the doorstep shooting the breeze. I am not the confrontational type, but that night I was there to call him out and bring our relationship to an open and honest end. After about fifteen minutes I said, "I saw you Craig. You love me, huh? That's a funny way of showing love."

He feigned ignorance to what I was talking about, and then I asked him where his shirt was and whose car was in his driveway. Just then Craig's blond visitor who had been waiting for twenty minutes in silent humiliation stormed out the front door, got in her Ferrari and drove away without speaking a single word. I wished him a good night and drove away.

Craig called me a few weeks later to see if I would help him pick out a suit for an upcoming job interview. I had foresight that he would ask me, and knew he intended to try to reconnect. I also knew that he would attempt to kiss me, and that I would slap him. I agreed to go along, wanting better closure than we had before. I told him he would have one hour at the store, that he needed to bring a friend so we weren't alone, and that I would drive myself. When our one hour concluded, he asked me for a ride to his motorcycle. As he got in the car he attempted to kiss me and I slapped him. That was the end of my relationship with Craig.

It was September by then and I moved into another unlisted apartment. My next bishop helped me to complete the paperwork for serving an LDS mission that my previous Bishop had helped me start. I took my desire to serve a full-time mission to the Lord and was told 'no'; that He had another type of church mission for me. I was also told that I would one day serve another type of mission that would begin in my early forties. I wasn't quite sure what that meant, but I knew it was not typical.

Still eager to serve the Lord in some capacity, I agreed to serve a church service mission. I submitted my papers in September of 1993. Within weeks, the First Presidency of the Church formally extended my relatively rare call to serve at the Missionary Training Center. I was set apart four months later following my 21st birthday in January of 1994, and served through November of 1995. The duration of my mission would be the traditional 18-month time frame, but I would serve 20 hours per week. That schedule allowed me to continue working and attending school with a reduced number of credits, and still allowed me to maintain a social life.

While serving as a missionary I had some special experiences and my gifts were expanded. I didn't have a companion like a traditional mission, and was free to attend church there as I wanted, which I did on most Sundays. I was also free to eat there as much as I wanted, but learned after a couple weeks that was not a good idea if I wanted to maintain my figure. Another benefit of serving there was the general reprieve from worldliness and the lust that was constantly around me at school, although the MTC was not completely without that.

I worked in the green room where they trained new missionaries, and the Telecenter, which was relatively new at the time. I was told to report any inappropriate behavior I witnessed, and especially men who had difficulty "locking their hearts." Unfortunately I did need to report a handful of elders over the course of my time there who asked for my phone number. But the majority of the missionaries I worked with were focused on the work.

On one occasion, I was involved in missionary discussion training with a group on non-English speaking missionaries. In the course of conversing with one another in our native languages, and me speaking in German, each of us experienced the gift of interpretation of tongues. The spirit was strong, and was the reason I was able to understand them. The spirit told me that my experiences with tongues in the MTC would play an important role in my future when I would share the gospel with all nations; a promise yet to be fulfilled.

I remember walking through the hallways of the MTC and "recognizing" couples and individuals, as in knowing them from premortality, understanding that I would have encounters with them in the future, and that many would participate in a future gathering. I also saw missionaries on the other side of the veil, and was interested to see some wore white robes, but most wore suits like the ones in mortality; I had the sense that there were various purposes and missions happening on the other side of the veil.

On occasion I was walking through the hallway and heard heavenly music, ever so subtly. While singing in church meetings I often sensed heavenly choirs joining in, but especially during the famous "Called to Serve" hymn. Whenever that was sung I saw the veil part and witnessed the missionary hosts of heaven joining in, as if they were getting their day of mission work started with their mortal counterparts. The power of the two choirs together was astounding.

*Our engagement photo in Provo, Utah
in February 1996. I was 23.*

CHAPTER SEVEN

A Dream Come True

Following the summer of 1995 as I began my junior year, I moved into the apartments at Condo Row in Kensington. My heart was very heavy with all that I had experienced during my previous year of school. I had casually dated numerous men in hopes of finding the faceless husband from my dream—my heart had been broken many times. The weight of my problems became almost unbearable.

In late August I was feeling the weight of the world, and took my broken heart to the Lord, at my usual place; the Provo Temple parking lot. I read scriptures until sunset, and then began pouring out my deepest feelings and emotions to my Heavenly Father. I made a commitment or a personal covenant with the Lord.

My prayer was in effect, "Lord, I would like to marry someone with the same standards I have, and who has saved himself like I have. If that isn't the plan, I will do whatever You ask of me. If You want me to remain single and celibate for the rest of my life, I'll do that. I will do whatever You want me to do, just tell me what it is. I commit my life to You because I love You."

It became a pivotal moment in my life. I left feeling the sense that the atonement was for everyone and that I needed to forgive

Craig and others, but that didn't mean I needed to date them or settle for someone with lower standards.

Two weeks later on a Friday night, my friend Kourtney and I were invited to a private get together at someone's apartment. It was a new semester and we didn't know any of the thirty or so people at the party. I had been working all day and was wearing a business outfit which made me a bit of a misfit in that college setting. I didn't bother freshening up and wasn't overly excited to be there.

As soon as we walked in I noticed two men across the room that looked familiar, as I realized they were from my freshman year three years earlier. They were whispering to each other as they looked straight at us, and I could tell they recognized me but weren't quite sure how. I said to Kourtney, "See those guys over there? They're totally checking us out."

Just then two other guys offered us some brownies and welcomed us. We scanned the room and the only guys that we were interested in were the two guys checking us out. Still, with all our dating troubles in the previous weeks we didn't care to start any new relationships that night. We only stayed long enough to play two games, lasting maybe half an hour.

During the first game we just watched. One of the guys, named Alex, began walking toward us and said to me loud enough for several people to hear, "Hey, did you used to live at Branbury?"

I replied that I hadn't lived there, and the conversation ended. Kourtney and I talked about possibly leaving, but decided to stay a little longer. The spirit then bore down firmly on me saying, "Stay and play the next game."

Prior to the party I had been given a visual of playing a game, which I began to realize was the second game we were about to play; I had even seen where I was supposed to sit, so I became curious and stuck around a little longer. In the game, the person to whom a certain question was asked had to answer truthfully using a "yes" or a "no." The person would draw a question from a pile and was required to read it out loud before the group. As I anticipated my turn I began to sense what my question would be, which would be "Is your spouse in the room?"

I was also given the answer, as my attention was directed to Alex's friend, Jeff. I hadn't even spoken to him yet, and it freaked me out a little bit. Just then I held my question in hand and read aloud, "Is your spouse in the room?"

I paused for a moment as blood rushed to my cheeks and then said, "Maybe."

My answer drew a simultaneous "oooohhh" from the crowd, who didn't even know me. I freaked out even more, but just brushed it off, and Kourtney and I left shortly after.

After we had left the building, the two guys who gave us brownies shouted at us from the balcony above, "Hey, there's a party later tonight at the Ho-house, you should come." The Ho-house got its name from a house down the road that was decorated in Christmas style with the word "Ho" on the roof. It was a well-known party and drew around 400 people.

Kourtney and I were tired, but decided to go. We went home and freshened up and got into more casual clothes, and went to the Ho-house thirty minutes later. We arrived to loud music, moshing, and idiotic college boys jumping off the roof. It was a stark contrast from the million dollar business clients I was working with only a couple hours earlier. The party was so big and continued to draw people from all over Provo.

Hundreds of people surrounded us. Before long it had gotten so out of control that local law enforcement responded to the scene to break it up. I felt repulsed and wondered what I was doing there and turned to Kourtney and said, "Let's go."

Everyone began to dissipate as policemen arrived. Then a strange thing happened: the crowd dramatically parted, creating a direct unobstructed view as I looked up and saw Jeff and a couple other buddies.

I looked at him noticing his big brown eyes, and the spirit whispered to me, "Walk up to him." I was told what to say, which is still funny to me to this day. I said, "I know this is going to sound like a total BYU line, but I know you from somewhere."

I knew where I knew him from, but wanted to help him connect the dots to our freshman year. We spoke for a few minutes as we brought it all together from our freshman year, and decided to walk the few blocks to his friends' condo to get reacquainted. After a few minutes Kourtney and I realized we needed to change some plans we had made with another apartment that night, so we decided to meet up at my condo with Jeff and Alex a little later.

After changing our plans, we slipped away for a few minutes and Jeff and Alex came by just missing us. We didn't connect again that night, and later found out they thought we had stood them up. But in the little time I had with Jeff that night, I began to remember more of him from three years previous as freshmen. I remembered seeing him around the dorms, at church activities, and in the Helaman Halls Cafeteria.

The next day, I had a morning brunch date planned, and an evening date planned with another guy. I called both of the guys up and cancelled, explaining that my roommate was going through a hard time and I needed to be with her, which was true. But the real reason was that I hoped to bump in to Jeff at the BYU football game that night, which I had been given foresight on. Until that time I had never cancelled a date in college.

As Kourtney and I were looking for our seats at the game, I heard a voice in my right ear calling, "Julie!"

I looked up and scanned the crowd. I couldn't tell exactly where it was coming from, but I heard my name two more times.

Then I looked in the direction I heard it coming from, and

I saw Jeff and Alex in the crowd about five rows up. Jeff was waving his arms at me trying to get my attention. I assumed it was Jeff who had been calling my name. I surprised myself by shouting back, "We'll come see you guys at halftime!"

I wanted to go talk to him so badly during the first half of the game, and was distracted the whole time. When half time came, Jeff and Alex were still right where they had been earlier. Unfortunately, Kourtney's boyfriend who had just broken up with her was only three rows down from us with another girl, which was more than she could handle. I hung out with Jeff and Alex during half time, and Jeff invited us over to their apartment following the game.

I really wanted to go, but Kourtney wanted to go home and get away from the pain of watching her ex-boyfriend of only three days. I struck a deal with Kourtney that I would leave the game early with her, if she would go to Jeff's apartment with me later.

We left the game and walked several miles to Smith's grocery store to get some Ben and Jerry's Ice cream and a pack of Red Vines. We walked a couple blocks from Jeff's condo and found a place under a tree to sit down. Even our stale red vines seemed to mock us and our broken hearts as we griped more about men.

I was conflicted. Only twenty-four hours earlier at Los Hermanos, I had sworn to Kourtney that I wanted nothing to do with men for six months. Now I was helplessly smitten by Jeff. My heart was skipping a beat as I thought of seeing Jeff in a few minutes.

We watched as the crowd from the football game dissipated and found their way back to their homes. Among that group was Jeff and Alex, who we noticed had about twelve girls trailing behind them. By that time it was late and we weren't feeling very social, especially for a group that size. We decided to go to their apartment, but only for a few minutes. We waited for an appropriate amount of time so as not to appear overly anxious to be there, which given the turn of events, we weren't.

We showed up, and as we walked in we found Jeff and Alex sitting on the couch with four girls on each side of them, having a great time. My immediate thought was, "If he thinks I'm going to show up and have anything to do with him with a bunch of twenty-year-olds hanging all over him, he's got another thing coming!" I had lost all interest in being there. Kourtney and I stayed long enough to offer Jeff's guests some stale red vines, and then we left.

The girls eyed me up and down wondering who I was, as Jeff stood up from the girl-covered couch and asked me to come in and stay awhile. Not interested in competing, I let him know we were tired and had church at 9 a.m.

The following Monday was an emotional day. On the way home from the mall, I had the thought to stop and see Jeff. I argued with myself thinking that I had been crying and my mascara was all over the place. But when I arrived at home I noticed a huge group of people there and didn't want to walk in on their fun in the middle of my emotions. I decided to go over to Jeff's place.

I was nervous about the impression I would give Jeff, having been emotional, and coming to his house at ten o'clock at night, but I felt the spirit had directed me to do so. I knocked on the door and was greeted by a guy on the other side inviting me to come in.

Jeff was lying on his stomach on the couch. He was wearing glasses and was reading one of his text books lying on the floor in front of him. Our initial chat turned into a serious discussion lasting three hours. I recalled Jeff's voice being deeply familiar throughout our visit. That night concluded when he asked me out on a double date the following Friday night

About two weeks went by, and I awoke on the morning

of September 28th, at 5:30 a.m. (a date that would become significant in my future). I had just had my usual dream, but it was different. I was peering over a canyon with my children and faceless husband standing to my left, only that time as my husband turned around to walk toward our car he had the face of a man I now recognized and had come to know the previous two weeks—it was Jeffery Rowe.

Finally, after seven years of waiting, seeking, and longing, my mystery man had an identity and my once darkened future became enlightened. It was also about two weeks following my sincere plea to the Lord for direction concerning my future husband in the Provo Temple parking lot.

Later, after we were engaged, I shared my dream with Jeff. It gave him great confidence and excitement for the confirmation I had received, and he was enthralled that I had dreamt about him. Early in our relationship he was excited about my gifts.

We saw each other every single day after that. I recorded in my journal following the first week together that we had talked for 35 hours in the first week alone. That was significant to me because our time together was based on deep and meaningful interaction and getting to know each other. I had bonded more deeply with Jeff than I had with any of the men I had dated up to that time.

On Jeff's birthday, October 7, we planned a date to Park City to the Oktoberfest. Later that night I treated Jeff to dinner at the Sundance Ski Resort. At the end of our date I professed my love to Jeff for the first time. His response to me was, "I am 83 percent sure I love you too."

I had been given foresight to his response so it didn't hurt my heart one bit, but I knew he loved me, and understood that was just how Jeff worked through his emotions. He would say to me and others then and later that he had never told a woman that he loved her before me, and he wouldn't use those words for anyone until he knew 100 percent.

Two days later I told Jeff I loved him as prompted by the spirit, to which he replied he was 86 percent sure he loved me in return. A day went by and I told him I loved him once more, and his response was, "I'm 90 percent sure I love you too." I just smiled, gave him a hug and a kiss, and waited upon the spirit. Three days later I was prompted again to tell Jeff I loved him, to which he replied "I'm 95 percent sure I love you too." I kissed him and said "I'm 100 percent sure I love you, Jeff." The next day I said "Jeff Rowe, I love you with all of my heart."

Jeff's love had increased to 97 percent. By day ten Jeff swept me off my feet of his own accord when he passionately said, "I am 100 percent in love with you!"

As things became increasingly serious with Jeff, I began to feel a new level of responsibility and practicality. I was level-headed and had often thought to myself that I intended to know very well, whoever I would marry in life.

I wanted to date for at least a year, see him sick, happy and grumpy; see him on every holiday and in every season, how he interacted with his family, the way he kept his home, and in as many situations as possible. I had no intention of marrying on a whim to a guy I didn't know well, whether I knew he was the right one or not. I had also known three girls from my freshman year of college who had gotten married, had children, and had already been divorced.

To complicate matters, I had college expenses and a potential wedding to pay for at a time when things weren't going well at work. My employers were squabbling over business practices and considered parting ways as business partners. One of them intended to have me become a business partner, which lead to awkward relationships at work.

I began having the sense that I would need to have Jeff meet my family soon. Even though I knew that he would be my husband and I loved him, I felt some apprehension at the thought. Meeting the family would be a new step I had never taken with a man before, and I began feeling the need to postpone our courting for awhile.

I thought a temporary breakup and dating other people might be a good thing to bring us more in line with each other while the dust settled on my work situation. The holidays were coming, and so I thought the timing would be right to call it off and maybe take a quick visit to meet families at some point over the holidays, then maybe we would pick things back up at the first of the year.

One day I mustered up all my courage and planned to go have a conversation with Jeff to break the news that I knew would come as a shock. I was sitting on his couch, ready to lay it all out on him, when two minutes into the conversation Jeff interrupted me as I rolled my eyes in irritation at him. He then leaned forward, pressed his finger to my mouth shushing me, and calmly said "Will you be my wife?"

It threw my plan to the wind and the next thing I knew we were kissing passionately through tears. Following our display of emotion Jeff pulled away and said "I take that as a yes?"

I later came to find out that the sudden pre-engagement was as much a shock to Jeff as it was to me, as he was simply following the direction he had gotten from the spirit. Then feeling nervous, and not realizing the magnitude of what he had just committed himself to, he nervously asked me not to reveal the news to anyone except my dad, as he jumped up and down in the apartment like a giddy school boy.

Soon thereafter we drove to Colorado so Jeff could meet my family and to celebrate Thanksgiving. A blizzard had rolled through and we just missed the gate closing the passes by ten minutes, or we would not have made it to Colorado that night. At that time my dad had custody of the children and was living in Colorado while my mom lived in an apartment down the road from them. My younger brother had just returned from his mission, and my youngest sister was about six years old. They were all in a bit of shock to see me not only with a man, but hanging all over him.

After Thanksgiving we went back to Utah and continued making wedding plans. In early December we went ring shopping and settled on a ring from Payne Diamonds in Provo. We got a good deal on a trade-in diamond that we picked out together. Jeff went and picked it up, so I knew he had it, but he hid it from me.

Three weeks later on December 27 during Christmas break, I flew into Kansas City to meet Jeff's family. As we approached the city I had visuals of future destructions caused by New Madrid seismic activity and foreign troops. There were casinos and factories on fire and the highways were breaking up amid some nuclear blasts. Downtown Kansas City and The Plaza were greatly damaged.

Jeff was there to pick me up from the airport. I had met both of his parents before and one sister, but meeting other family members would be a first experience. After I watched Jeff play a game of church basketball, we went to the Plaza in Kansas City, which I had seen destroyed hours earlier.

At 10:13 p.m. Jeff knelt down near one of the fountains and formally asked me to marry him. In addition to the ring, he took care of my Christmas present at the same time and gave me some Sunflower perfume, and the well-respected Truman G. Madsen audio tapes. We were welcomed to Jeff's family later that night by a fancy spread of food his mom had prepared. I spent four or five days and enjoyed my time with the Rowes.

Marriage planning didn't go for me like it did for many other women. With my mom out of the picture at the time, I had to plan my wedding largely by myself. We planned on getting married in the Denver Temple on April 24th following our next semester of school. But then realizing that most of our friends and a good number of extended family members lived in the Utah area, we changed the location to the Salt Lake City Temple, which fulfilled a childhood dream for me.

I received my temple ordinances three weeks before on March 28th. My Aunt Annette and Grandma Newman were sweet and went in together on a set of temple clothes for me. Normally a woman would receive her temple ordinances within a few days prior to being sealed in the temple, but I had received mine three weeks previously so I could attend my dad's second marriage.

We held our wedding reception at the Joseph Smith Memorial building the same day as our marriage. The rental expense for the space was mostly covered by contributions from my dad. Jeff and I covered all remaining expenses ourselves which included my dress, cake, flowers, photographer, and everything else associated with the reception. We were grateful to the four hundred and forty people who attended.

Jeff and I were the last people to exit the Joseph Smith Memorial Building, which closed at ten o'clock. Before leaving we went to get our things and to change our clothes in the tenth floor bridal room. After getting changed Jeff realized his brother had taken his car keys earlier, which left us stranded. We found a custodian who let us use a phone to call Jeff's dad so he could bring us our car keys. It was a dramatic delay to the alone time we wanted after a long day. We still laugh about that today. We were literally the last people in the building that night.

We stayed at the Crystal Inn that night before boarding our flight to Kansas City. The next morning, Jeff's dad and sister loaded all our wedding gifts into a storage unit in Salt Lake and drove Jeff's Volkswagen Jetta to Kansas so we would have a car when we came back after our honeymoon. We spent the next two nights at a condo near Table Rock Lake, in Lake of the Ozarks, Missouri.

We drove back to Kansas that Saturday in time for another wedding reception at 6:00 p.m. Unfortunately our outdoor reception moved indoors when a spring storm rolled through. Jeff's mom provided a nicely catered meal for about 150 attendees.

Married life was an adjustment for both of us, but we were happy. We spent our first summer as newlyweds selling door to door pest control in Texas. It was grueling work. I had seen the area many times in vision from high nationwide aerial views, but this gave me a chance to see it up close.

As Eastern Texas came into view, I had visions of hurricanes and tsunami's leaving devastation in their paths, as well as foreign troops coming in from the Gulf Coast. I saw illegal aliens moving in mass droves from the south on through Houston and the Dallas area after having breached the wall. I saw bombs and fires. Houston was greatly affected by the natural disasters and was in an absolute uproar. Dallas was overcome by marauders, thieves, and rapists going from house to house. I saw the corruption of supposed relief organizations

The contrast of working with wealthy clients in an air conditioned office to knocking doors in 100 degree heat was dramatic. As licensed technicians we sold pest control six days a week and worked ten to twelve hours a day. I spent that summer inspecting houses for roaches, fleas, mice, and other pests.

Having pest control frequently on my mind as I walked those neighborhoods opened up visionary experiences of the pestilences and plagues that would come in future days and how they would be spread. We made good money that summer, but it was disgusting.

Jeff and I were married in the Salt Lake Temple in 1996.

My college graduation from Brigham Young University.
I was 26, and Ethan was 10 months old.

CHAPTER EIGHT

Diversity in the Workforce

As our undergraduate experience began drawing to a close, Jeff and I started discussing our long term plans. Jeff wanted to go to graduate school in Topeka, Kansas, but our immediate concern was to make enough money to pay off some bills and establish a good savings to start our life together. This goal is what led us to the decision to work for Eclipse Marketing.

For the first six weeks we worked side by side and then realized we could be more effective if we split up. Being apart from each other was difficult but we found it more bearable using walkie-talkie's. Jeff worked on straight commission, and I took a base pay with commission, which gave us a more stable income than if we had taken the same payment plan. I later recalled the precarious situation it was walking around in a big city alone, but I felt heavenly protection.

For a young married couple we did well that summer, pulling in $25,000 between the two of us. Our last day of work was August 31st. We drove back to Kansas to pick up some things and then drove to Provo in time to move into our apartment and get settled in before school started.

Jeff had worked at a company called Rise prior to getting married, which was a facility that specialized in caring for physically and mentally handicapped individuals. I had just declared a major in psychology, and thought a job like Jeff's would be good experience. He helped get me a job at the same workplace, which was convenient. We were responsible for providing care for patients who were legally declared criminally insane. They required 24-hour care.

I was assigned to work with men between the ages of 18 and 30 years old. Many of them had struggles with pornography, and had run away from home and prostituted themselves. I only worked there one semester, because of an experience I had with a 30 year old man. One of the restrictions placed on that particular patient was that he was to be kept away from knives. One night prior to my shift, unbeknownst to me, he had somehow got a knife in his possession. He chased me down the street with it, and that was the final straw for me. I quit the next day.

I started working a second part-time job for the State of Utah at the Children's shelter with abused children. Its primary function was to take children from abusive homes that had been placed in state custody. I was working in an undisclosed location, and was not allowed to even tell my new husband where I was. The kids and their unfortunate situations melted my heart, and I wanted to adopt every single one of them.

That job required an associate's degree. I was responsible for caring after a two-year old girl and her six-month old younger brother. Professionals believe they had been left alone by their mother and had been living alone for 10 days. Authorities estimated that they hadn't had anything to eat but mustard and ketchup for four days. The poor little baby was found with feces in his diaper crying on the floor. When I went to put the little girl down for a nap she would use the only two expressions she knew, "Shut up, B----", and "F--- you."

There was a five-year-old boy who had been extremely sexually abused mostly by his father, but also his mother from the time he was 8 months old. The home he had lived in was near railroad tracks. My instructions were to keep him away from dolls and railroad tracks. Whenever he found a doll he would molest it. Any sight of railroad tracks triggered him. His situation was heart breaking; I loved him so much and have thought about him almost every day since!

In October of that first semester of school together, my aunt contacted me and Jeff, letting us know her son and husband were having some health issues which had led to some high medical bills. She was starting a travel consulting company at the time and needed some startup capital and knew Jeff and I had made out pretty well in our pest control job the previous summer. My aunt was a kind person. Grandma used to say to me, "She would give you the shirt off her back."

Jeff and I didn't know it at the time, but we were about to learn about ponzi schemes, firsthand. My aunt asked us to borrow some money to help with her bills, with a promise that she would pay us back with interest. Additionally, knowing that I had several years of professional experience in business management she sought me as a business partner in her travel company. We were both trusting and somewhat naïve college students and believed in serving others in times of need.

We loaned her $11,000 with the agreement that she would pay us interest, at her insistence. By and by she needed more money, so Jeff and I would give her $3,000 here, and $5,000 there. By April of 1997 when we left BYU we had loaned her $23,000, and our pest control savings had been wiped out.

By that time my aunt's travel business was up and running. I had met several of the people she was sending on trips who spoke highly of her. That boosted our confidence that our money was being put to good use with the promise of a good return on our investment. My aunt wasn't in a position to repay us in cash as she had agreed to, but she was able to send us on a vacation as a sort of "thank you" gift for the loan, and to buy our affections and confidence in her a little longer as she strung us along. It also served as a sort of celebration of completing our time at BYU. In June of 1997, we flew to the southwest Pacific, visiting Australia and New Zealand for nearly a month. It was on my aunt's dime, or so she said, but it was really our money.

My aunt was taking money from one client which funded the next client, and so on. I had other family members who were scammed as well. She pulled in additional funds by hopping from one bank to the next for loans, kiting the money; it was a classic ponzi-scheme which snowballed on her.

Her actions ultimately lead to a sentence of three years in the Idaho jail system, of which she served a year and a half. In the process of her litigation, she petitioned me for a letter that might help vindicate her in the court system. I felt betrayed and by that time knew I would never see our $25,000 again, so I couldn't bring myself to write the letter.

Years later my aunt died from various health complications. I found out later from a family member that my aunt had assumed that Jeff's father was well off financially, which apparently justified her in profiling and taking advantage of Jeff and me. When all was said and done, it left a $23,000 unpaid bill that fell squarely on Jeff, and which would become his burden for many years to come.

By April of 1997 Jeff had completed his Bachelor of Science in Psychology, and was accepted at Washburn School of Law in Topeka, Kansas. We lived with his parents for three weeks before our vacation to the southwest Pacific. An apartment in Topeka became available about the time we came back from our trip, and we were all ready to begin the next phase of our life as newlyweds in graduate school.

My college job of three years working at the investment firm piqued my interest in investing, which lead me to want to acquire my Series Seven, a financial license for stock brokers. I was told by the spirit at the time that wasn't the plan, so I got a temporary job working for Bank of America for five weeks while I looked for a more permanent job. During that time I was offered three other jobs, but took the one that interested me the most.

It was with a small business owner who designed and built house boats and speed boats. He was looking for someone who didn't' drink or smoke so they could keep a level head while driving and showing boats, which was one of the main reasons he hired me. I would be paid $30,000 plus commission. His business markets were mainly in Lake of the Ozarks in Missouri, Las Vegas, Lake Powell, and Florida.

I was excited to work there because I loved outdoor recreation so much. I became the office manager and executive assistant, and had the side benefit of being able to wash the speedboats they had on display at the office from time to time. I was also able to travel and help with sales.

My boss was forty years old and had just gone through a divorce. After about three weeks into it, he started hitting on me. One time he rubbed my shoulders, and when I called him out on it, he sent me to a massage therapist to help convince me that he didn't mean anything by it.

It came at a time when they were holding a big weekend boat show, and he didn't want me to quit so he paid me double time. I promised to help him out that weekend, and quit the following week in October of 1997.

At some point during that time period I began hearing the words, "You have a baby that is coming to your home." I wanted to have children but didn't feel ready. Our plan was to get Jeff through law school and get more financially stable first. I felt like I was still vulnerable from everything I had been through with the sexual assault, my parents' divorce, and the relationship challenges just over a year previously that I wouldn't be the best mother for a new baby. I also enjoyed being a working woman. I was motivated by the feeling of producing and staying busy.

I put off the continual promptings which seemed to increase over the next few months as I softened to the idea of having a child. I felt my grandfather Hanchett's hand on my shoulder accompanied by the words, "Julie, you need to prepare to have a baby."

The spirit kept pressing on me. In August I had a vision of a young man in his twenties delivering the same message, "You need to prepare to have a spirit come to your home." I didn't know it at the time but would later learn my visitor was the very child that would soon come to me. He visited several times.

Jeff and I took the question of whether or not to have a child very seriously. We found comfort and direction at such times by attending the St. Louis Temple, which was a five hour drive from our home and was a trip we made every other month. By December, the spirit had made it very clear that it was time for us to have a baby, so I went off birth control December 27th, on the one-year anniversary of our engagement. I became pregnant right away.

Jeff and I were ecstatic at the thought of having a new baby, although admittedly, I was terrified at the thought of being a mother. I was worried that with everything I had been through in recent years that I would "ruin" my children.

I had a sister attending a university in a nearby college town who was playing in an NCAA tournament. My family came out to watch her play and several of my family members stayed with us in our one-bathroom, two-bedroom apartment. That weekend I found out the sad news of our first miscarriage. I hadn't told anyone other than Jeff that I was pregnant yet, so telling them I had miscarried was out of the question. Besides that, I didn't want to ruin their fun weekend.

I did however decide to tell one of my sisters. When I shared the news of my miscarriage with her, I was met with the response, "Obviously Heavenly Father knows you're not ready to be a mother." Her words came to my heart like a dagger.

My miscarriage along with my sister's comment gave me an opportunity to reflect on how much I really wanted to become a mother, which was conflicted on the other hand by how afraid and unready I felt at the risk and responsibilities that come with motherhood. I sought God's forgiveness for my lack of faith and asked Him for another chance. I became pregnant again right away, and was given the due date of September 20th, which was later adjusted to October 24th, 1998.

Shortly after becoming pregnant I got another job working as the office manager for G&K Services, which was a uniform distribution company. I was the only woman among dozens of rough truck drivers. Within a week of working there, the assistant manager began hitting on me, and sexually harassing me. He was 43 years old, married and a father of 3, an ex-cop, and an ex-military man. I found his advances to be repulsive.

When news of my pregnancy became public knowledge my manager said to me, "Before you go and get big, fat, and pregnant, why don't you come and get a picture in a swimsuit on my Harley so we can make some money. We could probably get five hundred bucks." He said that half a dozen times, after propositioning me for an affair.

As my pregnancy progressed and I gained weight, he would "oink" at me as I walked by. His harassment and general mistreatment grew progressively worse as I refused his sexual advances. I think I could easily have filed a sexual abuse law suit and won, but never did. I needed the job and health insurance to pay for the upcoming baby and delivery expenses.

While working at G&K, I was eagerly working to finish my course work at BYU. I still had 47 credits to complete toward my Bachelor degree. From the time I left Provo I had been working on 38 credits of independent study. I took the other 9 credits at Washburn University in Topeka, which would later be transferred to BYU to complete my degree. This was all while I worked full time at G&K Services, and Jeff was attending graduate school and working as a European car mechanic.

I lost twenty pounds during my first trimester from throwing up as many as 15 times a day. During the second trimester I gained seven pounds, and then gained 28 pounds in the third trimester. Our first son, Ethan, was born October 29, 1998 at 7:13 p.m. and weighed 7 pounds, 11 ounces. I was overdue by five days when I was diagnosed with strep B positive and doctors decided to induce me. I had the baby blues for the first few days but things went smoothly after that. He was so cute it didn't take me long to get over my fears of being a mother.

As one of the oldest sisters of ten children, changing diapers and caring for little ones was old hat for me. I adapted to motherhood quite well and really loved having a baby of my very own. Ethan demonstrated natural physical abilities, crawling at 6 and a-half months, walking at 8 months, and running at 10 months old. I worked on my remaining independent study credits during the day and left home at 5:30 p.m. each night to attend Washburn University. Jeff adapted to parenting very naturally and he took care of Ethan on those nights I was doing school work.

Because we had given my aunt our savings we were required to get student loans and work in order to pay for graduate school and the new expenses of family life. Two weeks before Ethan was born I quit working for G&K to focus on my family. Four months following Ethan's birth I began working at Topeka Family Fitness Center, supervising the child care center and teaching children's fitness classes. It was a great job for a new mother because it allowed me to take Ethan along, avoiding the expense of a baby sitter. I also brought in extra income babysitting a neighbors' five year old daughter.

In May of 1999 I finished my 9 transfer credits at Washburn University, and in June I completed all my independent study credits with BYU. It was quite a feat considering all that had gone on that year, and it gave me a great sense of accomplishment. Education and graduation ceremonies were very important to Jeff, who insisted that I go back to Provo and walk that August. I was grateful to him for encouraging me to participate in the graduation ceremony. I walked away from Provo with a Bachelor of Science in Psychology.

With my school behind us and a little more time on our hands, Jeff and I began to have thoughts of having another baby. I had been receiving images in my mind of a baby girl, which Jeff and I felt would be our next child. A young man in his twenties appeared to my spiritual eyes with the same message I had received before Ethan's birth, "You have another baby that is coming to your home." I had assumed that my male visitor was an ancestor who came to announce the birth of the baby girl I had been seeing.

When I received my ultrasound and found out we were having a boy, I began to realize the visuals I had of a girl meant that we still had another child on the way following the current pregnancy. Sometime later I realized that the male visitor who had come to announce our next child had actually come to announce himself.

As the months of my pregnancy progressed Jeff was in his final semester of law school. He ultimately graduated in May of 2000, from Washburn School of Law. I was so proud of him as he finished in the top 25 percent of his class and was on the Washburn University Law Review, a unique opportunity for law students to publish scholarly work related to legal matters. I remember hearing in a male voice as he marched onto the stage during his graduation ceremony, "You and Jeff are in for some very difficult years related to his career." I was left with the impression that I needed to brace myself for upcoming trials and lessons we would learn together. Jeff continued working as a car mechanic for the remainder of that summer.

Jeff began applying to a number of law jobs, and ultimately landed a position with a law firm in Wichita, where we moved in August of 2000. We lived in a two-bedroom apartment on the west side of town for six months while looking for more permanent housing and saving for a down payment on our next home.

During that time, Spencer was born in the evening on December 5, 2000 at 6:38 p.m. He was nine days overdue, and was induced. I was strep B positive again, like I had been with Ethan, and almost had an emergency C-section due to complications. The nurses called for the procedure, and just at the last minute, Spencer decided he would rather come to the world naturally. He weighed 7 pounds 12 ounces.

The stable lifestyle we wanted for years would be short lived. Jeff worked at his new job from August to the following May when he was laid off. He came to see that his new employer hired him and a number of other young associates at a time their firm was experiencing a major change, which hadn't been made known to them at the time they were hired. Prior to signing papers on our home, Jeff went to the managing partner of the firm to let them know we were buying a new home and wanted to be certain that he would have a job. The managing partner looked Jeff squarely in the eyes and said, "I promise you will have a job," all the while knowing he would be laying Jeff off in the near future.

Jeff's hopes of settling into a new home and launching a new and prosperous career were dashed as he found himself unemployed with a little family to care for. The well-established law firm of 40 years filed bankruptcy and closed their doors.

That untimely event led to the pressure for me to find work to help make ends meet. I picked up a job with Hopewell Promotions selling jewelry. Within three months I had such high sales that I was asked to be the Midwest Regional Manager, involved hiring and training sales representatives. Jeff brought Ethan and Spencer to the department store where I worked so I could nurse Spencer, and would then spend a quick lunch break with me before I went back to work. In between all of that Jeff spent his days looking for work.

He soon found a job in August of 2001 working at the District Attorney's office in the Appellate division. In his ten months at the DA's office he wrote 60 briefs. In the meantime he continued looking for a more permanent long term job. In June of 2002 he was hired at a law firm in Overland Park, three hours north of where we were living at the time. Jeff moved there without me and lived with his parents for three months, while I stayed in Wichita to sell the house.

We did a lot of driving during those years, as we traveled back and forth on the weekends to be together, but also in our temple attendance. The frequent driving exposed me more keenly to a future disaster related to the New Madrid seismic zone which covers many of the states I lived and traveled in.

We were assigned to the St. Louis temple district, and tried our best to make the four hour drive on a quarterly basis or so to worship there. With all of our driving on those Missouri highways I was frequently exposed to visionary insights of destruction that will take place in that region in the future, particularly in regard to the New Madrid fault line, and flooding from the Mississippi and Missouri Rivers which I've seen will one day flow backward.

Every time we would drive in to the low-lying area surrounding the St. Louis temple parking lot I would see the temple flooded anywhere from two to ten feet of water, and would have visuals of the temple's ultimate destruction and decommissioned state.

On occasion I have been shown the Minneapolis temple, which is also in the path of the Madrid seismic zone, and saw that it would have a similar fate to the St. Louis temple. The Kansas City temple, which is my currently assigned temple, was built years later. While it is near the Madrid fault line, I've seen that it will survive the upcoming destructions.

In 2012 I only lived half and hour away and would attend two or three times per week. As I drove through the Independence, Liberty, and the Greater Kansas City area I would have visions of hundreds of people coming from the East, with white tents in many nearby cities. I've seen those events since I was in 3rd grade as we drove through as a family, and continue to have those visuals to this day.

We've also attended the Oklahoma City Temple over the years and while I believe it will also survive, it will suffer severe destruction related to the Madrid seismic activity and flooding, but also from marauders and civil unrest. I saw many bombs going off in downtown Oklahoma City.

Over the years my family and I have enjoyed traveling to Destin, Florida for a getaway location. On that sixteen hour drive I've been able to take different routes and have seen the southern end of the effects of the future New Madrid seismic event. That fault line passes through parts of Alabama and Georgia and I see floods wiping out the entire proximal area to that fault line.

As I looked out in the Gulf of Mexico, I saw Russian submarines, and saw Chinese and Russian troops then work their way north through the Gulf of Mexico. Interestingly after one of those trips in 2015, a friend let me know that Russian submarines had actually been discovered in the Gulf.

Returning to the story, I continued working my Jewelry sales job from home, and listed our house for sale by owner. That was at the time of the events surrounding September 11th, which complicated the selling of our home. There had been 10,000 layoffs in town so it was a complete miracle that we were able to sell within six stressful weeks from the day we listed it. We even managed to make a small profit, which came in as a handy down payment on our next home. It was a significant miracle and we recognized the hand of the Lord in it.

Two months prior to September 11, I had seen a number of tragic events in dream and vision, but shrugged them off as bad nightmares; dreams like that were not uncommon for me. But as 9-11 events actually unfolded to the world through major news sources, those dreams came back to my memory, only there were some differences in the way I had seen it in dream compared to the way I saw it unfold in the media. Those events triggered a dream I had in high school, of my dad working at the Pentagon and a bomb was detonated. I remember the fear it stirred up within me. I told my dad the dream and he tried to settle my nerves by explaining that such an act would have been a declaration of war, but he was high ranking enough that he wouldn't be deployed from such an event if it were to happen.

My mom was in New York City, twelve blocks away when the towers came down. I had several friends and family members living in D.C. and New York who were directly affected as well. Dad was working as the Notifying Chaplain in the Pentagon, but had been sent oversees the Sunday before on a last minute assignment. He was later responsible for notifying some of the families who were involved in the Pentagon incident. Because of what he told me several years before, I immediately recognized what I saw on television to be an act of war. Those tragic events struck a deep and personal chord in my heart and still do when I think of it.

After Jeff and I sold our home in Wichita, we moved to Overland Park, Kansas on October 13th, 2002. We purchased a side to side split level home and lived there for the next eleven years. Jeff got a job working as an associate attorney for a Medical Malpractice Insurance Defense firm, and I continued working in Jewelry sales since it was a work from home job. I had anywhere from 13-21 sales representatives working under me, and had hundreds of thousands of dollars worth of inventory at my house. It was a good job but I got a little burned out and quit selling in January of 2004.

By February of 2003, Jeff and I were talking about having a third child, which we believed would be a girl. I believed this in part because of my experience with thinking Spencer would be a girl several years before. We were concerned about the timing, because once again we were directed by the spirit to have another child at a time when our health coverage was unstable.

We took our question about the timing of our next pregnancy to the temple. When we walked out of the temple Jeff asked me what I felt about having another child, and I responded, "Well, if I'm not pregnant yet, I will be soon."

Jeff replied, "Yeah, that's exactly what I got too."

I leaned over, grabbed his hand and gave him a kiss. The next week I began throwing up, went to the doctor and found out that I was two weeks pregnant.

We had medical insurance, but because Jeff was new on the job, the maternity portion hadn't kicked in yet. We paid out of pocket as we went along through the maternity doctor visits, and we were able to have all pregnancy and delivery expenses paid in full by the time our baby arrived. I had just turned 31 in January of 2004, and Aubrianna was born one week later on January 13. She weighed exactly 8 pounds.

Things began to heat up at Jeff's job with Medical Malpractice Insurance Defense. A change in partnership at the firm was in progress, and the firm had just lost the largest defense case in the nation which created the need for layoffs. Naturally they began with the most recent hire's. I discerned that Jeff's boss, the managing partner, was having an affair at the time and was given a full visual of the woman he was sleeping with. One day while Jeff was in the elevator having a conversation with his boss, Jeff said something to the effect of "You need to be careful who you trust. If someone is having an affair, you know they can't be trusted."

When Jeff told me about their conversation I said, "Jeff, you have to be careful what you say. He's having an affair!"

He asked me where I had received that information, challenging me a bit, to which I said three times, "I've seen that he's having an affair."

Three months prior at the company Christmas party, that same manager had gotten completely drunk. Jeff and I were the only sober employees in attendance. As Jeff's associates and their wives were standing around getting ready to leave the party, Jeff went to get the car, leaving me for a few minutes to say goodbye. While he was away the managing partner came to give me a hug, and completely out of sorts buried his head into my chest. Meanwhile his intoxicated partners laughed and cheered him on.

Several months later the managing partner was forced out of the partnership, but by then it was too late for Jeff, who had been laid off in April 2004. The layoffs and politics surrounding his previous jobs caused Jeff to rethink his profession, but by that time we had upwards of $80,000 in graduate loans, over $20,000 of which was from my Aunts' ponzi scheme several years previously.

We found it difficult to leave the profession with that kind of investment, and with the need to pay off those loans. Jeff remained unemployed for the remainder of that summer. His several jobs in only a few years drew unfriendly criticism from friends and family. Some misattributed his unfortunate employment circumstances to his lack of skill as a professional.

The truth was that Jeff had frequently been hired in precarious work situations, working under business squabbles and partnership splits. Jeff is a highly intellectual man with solid integrity, and in some cases was laid off due in part to his refusal to participate in or condone unethical practices. The difficulties that came from his unfortunate work experience to that point were only a precursor to the kinds of challenges we would face together in only a few months time.

Our family in 2007 in Overland Park, Kansas.
Ethan was 8, Spencer was 6, and Aubrianna was 3.

A family vacation in Destin, Florida in July 2013.

CHAPTER NINE

A Dramatic Answer to Prayer

Jeff and I and our three children spent a lot of time outdoors during the summer of 2004. I was also in charge of a sibling family reunion for my family that July. A couple weeks later we spent the week at Lake of the Ozarks State Park in Missouri, camping and playing in the water with some friends.

Five weeks later on a Saturday night in September of 2004 I was having heart pain over the hurting relationships in my life. My parents and some other family members were the main sources of that pain, but some of it had come from other personal challenges. It felt to me like spiritual daggers had been placed deep within my heart, and I prayed and asked the Lord to remove them.

Jeff had left town to attend his grandpa's funeral in Idaho, and it was the first time in our marriage of eight years that I had any real time to myself. It was nearly midnight, the kids had all gone to bed, and I knelt down for three hours in prayer and supplication to the Lord. I begged, cried, pleaded, and said in effect, "Lord I hurt, I would do anything to get rid of these daggers in my heart, please remove them, my heart hurts, it is broken, and I can't do this anymore."

I went through dozens of people in my life that I held

heartache over, asking for healing and charity, and then I spoke the most life changing words of any prayer I had ever said: "Please bless me with charity. I will do anything for the gift of charity, even if you will give me an Alma the younger experience, or a King Lamoni experience, I will do whatever it takes to get that gift."

Little did I know that I had just said the words that would initiate an experience triggering my premortal responsibilities and agreements. The gifts I had known throughout my life intensified that night as I had more powerful past, present, and future visionary experiences.

The following Tuesday I began feeling ill with flu-like symptoms, experiencing vertigo, diarrhea, and nausea. I was vomiting so much that I couldn't keep water down. Ultimately my illness landed me in the hospital where I had a life changing near-death experience which is described in my book, *A Greater Tomorrow*, published in 2014.

It was later medically confirmed on my lab results that I had Epstein Barr virus. I was also told and shown by the spirit that I had Lyme disease, but that was not medically confirmed until 2010, after years of doctor visits and half a dozen auto-immune diagnoses.

Ethan was scheduled to have his first field trip at school and I had to miss it, which broke my heart. Jeff went with him instead. Jeff and his mother took over all the cooking and cleaning, and housekeeping while I recovered. Aubri was still nursing and because I was hospitalized she was weaned cold turkey, which added to the stress. For the next year and a half I struggled with depression and health challenges. Diarrhea, vomiting, and joint pain became my norm, which I've learned to just live with to this day.

My daughter Aubri was eight and a-half months old when I was admitted to the hospital. As I have reflected back upon my life with Jeff and the timing of things, I realize that if we had waited any longer to have Aubri, due to the complications with my health, she very likely would not have been born to our family. Each day since, I have felt gratitude that we listened to the spirit and decided to have our children when we did.

My near-death experience was a turning point in my life for many reasons. It was a culminating point in my physical health, which began to deteriorate rapidly thereafter. I had a deeply intensified witness of God, and His Plan of Happiness, having seen the world from the beginning of its creation, to its end following the Millennium.

I was given experiences that would leave me with a greatly expanded sense of time and space, a sense that mortals simply cannot understand until having the experience themselves. I quickly learned that anyone I told would find my experience too preposterous to believe, which wasn't anything new. I had learned to keep my visionary experiences to myself throughout my whole life. It was just that now my spatial, temporal, metaphysical, and emotional spectrums had been greatly expanded beyond mortal comprehension.

A few weeks following my near-death experience I began to share some of the things I had experienced on the other side of the veil with Jeff. I was still astonished by the intensity of the color of the flowers, heavenly music, angels, and mansions in heaven, just to name a few things from the enormous array of expanded and heightened sensory experiences I had. My attempts to describe those experiences to him didn't resonate, as evidenced by his reply, "I feel like I've lost my wife forever."

I knew he had witnessed me in conditions of psychosis, speaking with speech impediments as I recovered, and my sometimes odd behavior as I readapted to my two-dimensional life from the multi-dimensional magnitude of my near-death experience. I knew my logically minded attorney of a husband went to the defense of reason and science, before the voice of emotion and the magnificent splendor I had experienced on the other side of the veil. I felt he listened to the voice of mortally trained professionals who had declared me mentally ill. It broke my heart, and I felt helpless to convince him or anyone what I had experienced.

I felt my visionary gifts and prophetic experiences I had received throughout my life were not well received. My gifts were being rejected by the one I wanted to understand me the most. With Jeff's very bright mind comes skepticism and cynicism. But despite his strong intellectual side, he has an incredibly big heart and loves me deeply. I have never questioned his love for me, but his inability to see and feel and understand me broke my heart. Despite losing me to mental illness, as he viewed it, he continued to love me through it all.

In order to help with the negative effects of my mental health, doctors prescribed a very high dose of a particular medication that would cause strong side effects. As Jeff and I were both psychology students with some understanding of the effects of heavy drugs, and through some general counsel from our pharmacist, we decided against taking the drug.

In October and November of that year, I had two more near-death experiences that I have never spoken of publicly. They were not near the magnitude of my experience in September, but they were special in their own right.

In October, I was having complications from Lyme disease and the Epstein Barr virus. I was in my home when two women from the other side came to visit me in a very specific healing capacity. I recalled slipping to the other side of the veil and receiving some instruction, but then came back and the experiences were taken from my memory. When Jeff recognized my serious condition he took me to the Olathe Medical Center in Kansas.

I stayed there on the women's medical floor for one night, and when doctors couldn't discover what was wrong with me, they sent me to the Shawnee Mission Medical Center. While there I slipped through the veil and two female ministering angels provided me with specific healing. In that experience I learned certain doctrines and more concerning my future mission.

Over the next two days, medical professionals ran tests to find the cause of my condition with no success, and ultimately sent me home. I was sent back to the hospital for another five days where I slipped out of my body again, that time experiencing darkness on the opposite side of the spectrum which became a living hell. When I couldn't take any more I begged Jeff to go home.

As we frequently traveled to hospitals for medical treatment I had many visionary experiences of the destruction that would come on the highways and cities in the wake of the large Madrid seismic activity. For example, as I approached the Kansas City airport on highways 29 and 635 I always saw, and continue to see, a portion of the highway near the casino and factories that will be completely impassible from the earthquake. But on most of those trips my visions had a stronger focus on the other side of the veil, where a very real spiritual warfare was underway among light and dark forces.

For the next month I had migraine headaches, psychosis, and paralysis. Having previously rejected the doctors prescribed dose, and having gone through a great deal of stress himself the previous weeks and months, Jeff found himself on bended knee in our kitchen one night, begging me to take the medication. I submitted to his will. It caused tremors and dizziness, and I could barely walk. I had perpetual diarrhea and vomiting, experienced depression and suicidal thoughts, but the medication seemed to help in stabilizing me in other ways. I gained 45 pounds in two months which compounded my self-image issues.

Despite my challenges, my overall health was in good hands. I continued to visit my primary care doctor, and I had a friend who was a stay at home mom but was also a Chiropractor. She would come to visit a few times each week. Trained in eastern medicine, she did acupuncture and energy work on me three times a week from October to February.

It was the first time I had seen energy work done on this side of the veil. She was able to diagnose my liver as the primary source of my infection, and helped with treatment. My primary care doctor provided a second witness that my liver was infected and that the infection had gone systemic, which meant the Epstein Barr virus had infected me from head to toe.

My psychiatrist was named Deborah. I worked with her for 8 and a-half years. She started seeing me three weeks following my September near-death experience, and diagnosed me with Bi-polar 2. Shortly after she began seeing me she was admitted to the hospital herself for a triple bi-pass surgery. I confided in her after a couple weeks and let her know much of what I had seen during my near-death experience over the next two months.

Deborah shared with me that during her triple bi-pass, she slipped to the other side of the veil and had her own simple but sweet experience. She told me that she had "seen the hand of Jesus."

Additionally she told me that she believed my experience, and all that had happened to me. She told me that she didn't believe I was truly bi-polar, but that was just the medical term for someone with some of my symptoms.

Deborah was a special woman. After she had seen me for six years, she said she was prompted to learn Israeli Hebrew and she went to Jerusalem where she learned about her Jewish ancestry, which included some who had escaped from Nazi Germany. She was a deeply spiritual woman of another faith than me, and said of herself that she was a "God-fearing woman."

I loved her very much, and was touched by her experience. She died in April of 2012 from health complications. After her passing she came to visit me a few times from the other side. I didn't see her with my physical eyes, but felt her presence and smelled her perfume during those visits.

As a side note, I have often experienced the gift of spiritual smell, which has included the distinct and familiar smell of my Grandma Hanchett. While touring the castles in Germany I smelled dirty dungeons, death, blood, smelly feet, torture and lust. At other times I have smelled dirty shoes, cigarettes and cigars, body odor, alcohol, coffee, and even chocolate.

By February I had been taken off medication, and stayed off it until I experienced another flare-up with the Epstein Barr virus. We were on a two week vacation in Colorado and Utah during the month of July. The Wasatch region has a tendency to trigger my spiritual senses, dreams, and visions which become extremely heightened. Such was the case at the family reunion we attended over the 4th of July, at the Cherry Creek KOA. I was sensitive to the good and bad people there, and sensed the seismic activity of the past, present, and future. I also sensed the lust energy of a relative who had impure relations with his family members.

The heightened energy combined with the Epstein Barr virus triggered me into a psychosis that night, leading to an out of body experience. I was in my mom's house where family members cared for me and brought me food while I was having intense visionary experiences, and spoke in what sounded like nonsense to anyone passing by, speaking of celestial worlds and visitors from other places.

To this day I still have family members who believe I am just crazy. They have never taken the time to really ask questions or find out what happened to me. I wasn't bothered that they witnessed me in that state of mind, but it does bother me that they have never taken the time to ask me about the experience, or my condition. I think they are too afraid to ask and are frankly guilty of passing judgment without having sought understanding.

Jeff eventually took me to the University of Utah, which was my first time being there in body, but I had seen it in spirit since the time I was a junior in high school. I believed it to be by divine design that I was being treated there, as I was shown that a huge future earthquake would have its epicenter very near that location.

The hospital contacted Deborah in Kansas and she called in a prescription for me. Jeff needed to get back to work, so his parents drove from Kansas to pick me and the kids up and to drive us home. Within a couple days I regained my composure. Meanwhile, Jeff had just started a new job, was still awaiting a paycheck, was stressed out by medical bills, handling our children, as well as his ill wife. This came at a time when Jeff was having concerns over his employers' unethical practices. After a year and a half of working there, he and a co-worker decided it was time to leave. Jeff became the brains behind a financial services company.

We met with Jeff's coworker and his wife to discuss the possibility of starting the business Jeff had envisioned. At first I resisted the idea, but eventually agreed, believing that supporting Jeff was the right thing to do. I had plenty of business experience and Jeff was adventurous. We formed the partnership with our friends who provided the capital to get it going. Jeff and I held 49 percent ownership in the business, since our partners contributed 75 percent of the startup capital. We started the new business in 2006, and I had a strong feeling that it wouldn't end well.

Jeff and his coworker had entered a no-compete agreement with their previous employer, which led to an ongoing lawsuit for the first year of running our new business. That employer had breached his contract and owed Jeff and his partner thousands of dollars in unpaid commissions and the lawsuit was thrown out.

Jeff was the president of the company, which provided a healthy stretch to his professional skills. I was able to see some of his spiritual gifts as we encountered new challenges together that required heavenly guidance and inspiration, which brought us closer together.

For those two years we lived mostly on credit cards while the business was established. In the meantime our partners began embezzling, ultimately stealing the business right out from beneath us, since we had the smaller share in it. We had a compelling case with the law but were told by the spirit to simply walk away from the situation.

Jeff then went to work for Edward Jones as a financial advisor. I studied for and received my Kansas real-estate license and began learning about real-estate investing. I purchased two homes with the intent to fix and flip. Ultimately, I was conned by the men who sold me the houses, so instead of being able to flip them for the profit I had originally hoped for, I was forced to turn them into rental properties.

When the economy tanked in 2008 my renters were unable to pay their rent and refused to move out. That left us paying both mortgages out of our own pockets, eventually forcing us to file for short sale on both rental properties. Those transactions lead us further into debt, and we were advised to declare bankruptcy which we refused to do. We experienced marital strife during those stressful months, but were able to work through it. I picked up another hobby job selling jewelry and began working as a Para Professional in an elementary school.

Jeff was offered another job working for Creative Marketing where he worked for five years. Our two boys were in first and third grade, and Aubri was in pre-school in the afternoons, so my mother in law watched Aubri while I worked. Having Jeff's mother so near allowed me to work without requiring daycare, which we were grateful for.

In December of 2010 I was experiencing back and neck problems that were linked to my large chest size so doctors highly recommended that I receive a breast reduction. The procedure took place in the morning, and went smoothly. I was scheduled to stay the night at the hospital and was told to expect a three week recovery. By 3:30 in the afternoon doctors discovered that a blood clot had developed in my left breast.

Things progressively worsened, and after an hour I was in critical condition. They scheduled me for an emergency surgery to remove the clot. I waited in the Emergency Room until 11:00 when the procedure took place, all the while I was experiencing intense pain as my breast continued to swell. It nearly burst the stitches that had been put in place earlier that morning.

The same anesthesiologist who had worked on me the first time was still on duty, and prepared me for a second surgery. The pain I was in had once again caused my spirit to separate from my body. I looked down and saw my body on the operating table, and heard the doctors discussing the seriousness of my condition. The veil was thin, and I saw a number of future national events and gained further insight into my future mission. I was also attended to by the same women who had cared for me during my previous near-death experiences.

Despite the seriousness of my condition I was given a strong sense of confidence and was totally at peace. When I awoke, I recalled my experiences on the other side of the veil, and the miracle it was that I had been attended to by those caring women. I was in pain from being opened up twice in the same place in less than a 24-hour period, and had nausea. Recovery was more painful and took longer than I anticipated. I left with a sense of gratitude for modern medicine and skilled medical professionals, but would never willingly go under the knife again.

Following a three week recovery, I resumed work as a Para in early January. I worked from 8:30 a.m. until 3:10 p.m. when it was time to pick up my boys from school. Then I would drive to pick Aubri up from my mother-in-law's home. I worked as a Behavior Disorder Para Professional teaching K-3 elementary students in Kansas, with the most difficult students in the region.

One kindergarten child had an incredible ability to climb right up the cinder brick wall like a monkey. Another student could pick up a desk and throw it across the room. There was another child who often removed his pants and urinated on me when he was unhappy with me. But despite the unruly behavior and foul language of the children, I felt compassion for them and their personal circumstances, which often broke my heart.

As much as my coworkers and I tried to teach the children basic reading and mathematics, for all intents and purposes it was a babysitting job, and we called our day a success if we could get each child to complete a few math problems and go home without serious injury. The head behavioral disorder teacher had worked in her position for 20 years in those conditions. I had great respect for her.

I had been working at that job for one year when I decided to begin working toward a teaching license and Masters of Education degree at the University of Saint Mary in Leavenworth Kansas. I attended the Overland Park campus. I continued working with those children for another two years while taking night classes. I completed my student teaching in the spring of 2011. During that time I worked as a substitute teacher for two years in three different school districts teaching students K-12, including special education. During my experience I taught most subjects, and worked with children who had every behavioral disorder listed on the books. While it was difficult, it gave me great experience and an opportunity to develop skills with youth and challenging children. I loved working with youth.

In May 2013, Jeff got a new job in Arizona. We hadn't sold our home and the kids were still in school, so he lived in Arizona by himself the first few months while I put our house on the market and the kids finished the school year. The kids and I went to Utah and Colorado to visit my family while our home was on the market. Jeff came back to pick us up in July and we moved into our new home in Oro Valley, Arizona. Our house sold in September.

We lived on a gorgeous golf course in that beautiful desert oasis for 15 months. Jeff really loved his job, was compensated well, and we felt truly happy there. We didn't know life was about to take us for another roller coaster ride, as visions and reminder dreams of my 2004 near-death experience returned with greater intensity. I began to feel the weight of the understanding I was given and the spirit continually reminded me that the time would soon come when I needed to make my story known.

With each of those dreams and visions came understanding that I had volunteered for this 'mission', before I had set foot on the earth. But the more powerful reminder of the public phase of my mission came on the nine year anniversary of my 2004 near-death experience. September 28 and 29 are dates that have come to have significant meaning.

On October 15, 2013, Jeff and I went out to eat. I got very sick, feeling the weight of the burdens that had been placed upon me physically, emotionally, and spiritually. I went into the restroom and fell to the floor and verbally called out, "Why?" to which came the unequivocal reply from the spirit, "Don't ask why. Ask how and what. Ask, 'What am I to do, and how am I to serve?'"

Then I heard the words, "I love you." That impression was followed up over the next few hours with more answers about sharing my story, lessons I had learned previously, and certain promises that would be mine if I remained faithful.

Through the pain and difficulties of the previous nine years I had often asked the same question of "Why?" But I had also been given impressions, thoughts, and voices of those from the other side who reiterated their love for me, and reassurance that things would be okay. Sometimes they would give explanations of specific action items toward writing, or the purpose of various ailments that I had been experiencing. But through my experience on the bathroom floor I knew the time for self pity had ended and it was time to get to work.

Ever since my near-death experience I had seen myself writing books and speaking publicly, and those visions continued to intensify. They helped me to develop a strong conviction that the time to write a book and carry out those speaking engagements had come.

I felt a deepened sense of the things I knew were facing the United States in the near future and I couldn't keep it to myself. I felt like I would be a terrible person if I didn't "warn my neighbor," as the scriptures say. My deepened sense of responsibility made me nauseous as I threw up on the bathroom floor. I often feel nauseous when having overwhelming emotional experiences.

I soon received direction from the spirit to get certified with Dr. Bradley Nelson's Emotion Code program. I enlisted in the course and eagerly and swiftly advanced through the program between October and January. Within three weeks of receiving my certificate and having the hope of using my new credential as a business woman, I was instructed very clearly that I was not to use my certificate for profit at that time, but that it would be used for other reasons.

While living in Oro Valley I wrote and published my first book, *A Greater Tomorrow*, and my second book *The Time is Now*. Because I had gone public with my story, stalkers and death threats began to emerge. Many people gossiped and spread false rumors about me.

Once we had settled in our home in Iowa, someone in the LDS Church had released a letter directed to Church Education System personnel reminding them that unauthorized books should not be used in teaching seminary classes, and they used my book as an example of the kind of sources that should not be used. While I agreed with the message of that letter, it caused a great flurry of personal attacks and created a large group of haters within the church toward me.

At around the same time, some anti-Mormons were actively promoting messages that were contrary to church teachings, and each of them had been excommunicated. In the meantime, I was active in my church meetings and temple attendance, and my faith and testimony burned brightly as a member in good standing. There were those who tried to put me in the same category as those who had apostatized, but their accusations were false.

In the year that had transpired since my experience in the restaurant bathroom I had known of the impending persecution and controversy surrounding my story. In the fall of 2013 the spirit made known to me that we would be living in Arizona for less than a year. In March of 2014, the spirit made it known to both Jeff and I that Jeff would be getting a job in Des Moines, Iowa.

Jeff was at the top of his career. He had a good salary and loved his job, which was a good fit for his professional skill set. The benefits were great and he had been offered a company trip for two to the Mediterranean. We had no reason to leave.

Jeff applied for a job in May and was hired to start work in October. When he told his employer, Jeff was counter-offered a pay raise of $75,000 to stay, but he had received his witness from the spirit in March of 2014 that we were to move to Iowa, so he knew his response before they made the offer. He took a substantial pay cut to do so. We told friends we were going back to the Midwest to be with family, which was true, but the reality was that the Lord was asking it of us.

As movers came to pack up our home, I was busy completing my second book. On October 15, the day we arrived to our new home in Iowa, *The Time is Now* went to press, one year from the time I had my experience in the restroom.

Prior to moving back to Iowa, I was given the instruction to go "unlisted." I began to see that the benefits of living unlisted in the middle of the country in an obscure town had its advantages. It would give us some measure of privacy and security. It would also create a greater convenience for the next portion of my mission, traveling across the United States from a central location to various speaking engagements.

Before leaving Arizona we took a family trip to the Grand Canyon in March of 2014. While there I saw in vision a time when many would flee to the Canyon seeking safety from foreign troops, and I saw torrential rains and other extreme weather conditions. When driving through Flagstaff I was shown a bit about the huge drug problem that exists there, and saw that it is and will be in the path of a major trafficking corridor. I was told specifically that Phoenix is the largest city in the nation for human trafficking, and would become the capital in the world, and that my mission would eventually become involved in combating that terrible problem.

Two days following our arrival in Iowa, I went to bed and had a night vision of myself on Fox News, the Today Show, the Glenn Beck Program, and several other radio and TV shows. I awoke in a panic, and feeling overwhelmed I broke down in tears. Through that experience it was made very clear that I would have another book that would reach a much larger audience than my first two books. I understood the media storm I had seen in my night vision would follow an event they had given me called, the Wasatch Wakeup. As I began to use that term, my blog viewers began having questions concerning that event. I posted two blog entries describing the event as it had been shown to me, which are captured below:

April 21, 2016
"The Wasatch Wake Up"

When is the Wasatch Wake-Up Earthquake? Everyone wants to know. I don't discuss timelines here, but my feelings are that the Wasatch "Wake-Up Earthquake" is very soon. We have a few intense days ahead of us. I see a whirlwind of activity along the Wasatch Front. When this earthquake hits, you will see the media swirling, the headlines screaming, the believers and non-believers alike discussing this earthquake.

When a major earthquake hits the Wasatch Front, many people will think they have made it through "The Big One." What they don't realize is that the really, truly big one is yet to come - the likes of which have never been seen or felt in Utah in modern days. That one is not imminent. It will be after the U.S. presidential election and the upcoming national economic troubles.

Will this first "Wake Up Earthquake" be enough for people to recognize, understand, and discern what has happened? What will it take for people to turn their lives over to the Lord, trust in His plan and his tender mercies, and ask in faith? What will it take for people to repent, forgive, forsake, and recommit to their beliefs?

What does "soon" mean? Soon could mean tomorrow, or next month, or next year, but to me the message is clear: "The Wasatch Front Earthquake is soon. Get ready for the whirlwind. Ground yourself in the knowledge you have, and the truths you know. Have faith. Trust the Lord. Get ready for additional transitions and watch the miracles unfold."

-- Julie

April 27, 2016
"What is the Wasatch Wake Up?"

I see a literal wake-up call earthquake. As in, I see the earthquake on the Wasatch Front happening early morning around 4-4:30 am until about 6-6:30 am with aftershocks.

I see a warm sunny day with rain and an unexpected cold front that brings in a quick snow fall to the valley the night before. I see green grass and patches of melting wet snow, wet grass, no ice, no sleet, no shoveling. I see melting snow and wet roads from rain. I see that the Wasatch Wake-up is a literal wake-up call. Several people are awakened as they feel the trembling of the earth beneath them and items fall around them. I see startled faces and excitement. I see scrambling for glasses, flashlights, shoes, and clothes. I see affects at the airports, the campuses, the highways, the airbases, the real estate along I-15 etc., crashing glass buildings. I see a wake-up earthquake with reports of aftershocks for several days. I see hospitals, schools, college campuses and housing affected and I see a wake-up that leads to a media whirlwind and a domino effect.

I see power outages, help needed, rescues, and escapes. I see faith shaken and faith awakened. I see hearts softening and healing happening. I see refugees, rescue, service, repair and replenishment. I see shelves shaking and emptying and charity extended.

I see that as expected, Wasatch Earthquake is yet a warning shake that will wake up several who are disaffected, disenchanted, distracted and disengaged. I see Wasatch Waking up and realizing that the Time is Now.

A portrait taken in Kansas in April 2017.

CHAPTER TEN

The Message Goes Public

From my near-death experience of 2004 I was left with the understanding that I would need to make my experience public in nine years. While the details of how that would happen were not clear at the time, I understood that it would involve writing a book, and holding public speaking events. But the thought of taking anything personal to the public went against my upbringing, and my nature. Now that I was living in a secluded place in Iowa, I was perfectly suited to plan and prepare for the public life that I would soon submerge myself into.

Book Writing

In 2013 while living in Arizona, I began to receive the understanding through dreams and day and night visions that I would hear from my publisher some time after the first of the year, but distinctively heard the word, "February."

I had been shown many of the events in the life of my future publisher, including his own near-death experiences, scenes from his college years, his courting and marriage, his children, his company and the sacrifices he had made to keep it going, and other events from his life. Then in my 2013 collapse in the bathroom I was given additional scenes of his life. I was told and shown by the spirit that he had been shown and told about me.

Knowing it was time for me to go public with my story, I rejoined a social media group on a preparedness website online. On that website, users create an alias for themselves, and I joined with the alias name of "fellowdreamer."

My publisher, Chad Daybell, was also a member of that website, which is how we came in contact with each other. Chad rarely visited the site, but had felt prompted to check it before going to work, and he saw my post asking if anyone knew someone who could help me publish my story.

Chad responded that he owned Spring Creek Book Company and would be interested in talking with me. Within a week we had agreed to publish my book *A Greater Tomorrow*, and it was released in May 2014.

Radio Talk Shows

Given the choice between writing about my experiences verses speaking about them, I prefer speaking any day! I've been told more times than I can remember that for many who read my books, my written accounts served as a sufficient voice of warning on their own, but listening to me speak on the radio or in person was more convincing to many of my listeners.

Mills Crenshaw

The radio shows and speaking events were intense, but they were enjoyable for me—especially after I got used to being in the spotlight. The public speaking portion of my mission began with the first of what would become four interviews with the late Mills Crenshaw.

Mills was a popular AM radio conservative radio talk show host in Utah. As a first time radio guest and despite my strong witness that it was now time to go public, I was still grappling with the idea of even going public with my story at all. I felt great anxiety. Thoughts of my upbringing, which frowned upon the thought of sharing personal experiences publicly, often surfaced. Going from my eleven years of near silence to a relatively major radio station was a contrast for me to say the least.

A number of interesting events came from Mills' interviews. Following the first in-person show, I walked out the door where I was met by a group of people who were interested in visiting. That was new for me.

The third interview was conducted on November 13, 2014, by phone and was largely centered on the recent release of my second book, *The Time is Now.* Mills conducted a fourth radio show that was similar to the other shows, with some new added insights, each serving to establish my name and create awareness in thousands of people. Mills took some criticism for covering my story, which stirred up controversy mostly among Utah Mormons.

Kate Dalley

Throughout the 18-month publicity mission I made a few appearances as a guest speaker on the Kate Dalley Show. Kate was great to work with, was respectful to me, and our friendship really deepened through our experiences together.

During the January show while off the air, I told Kate that she would one day work for Blaze Radio, which Kate had no connection with at the time. It was a far cry for me to say it, but the inspiration to say so came pretty strongly. A short time later, The Blaze contacted Kate through Facebook and selected her as one of their talk show hosts.

Kate took a lot of heat over covering my story. She became a good friend to me and I asked her to write the foreword on my third book, *From Tragedy to Destiny*, which she did. She is a strong, brave woman, who courageously speaks out in defense of freedom and liberty. I believe we knew each other premortally and must have been good friends.

I made some other public appearances on some less known but still very purposeful shows—two of which were in webinar format. We recorded ten to fifteen hours in total together. Additionally, I made an appearance on the Steve Mitton Radio Show for an hour in January 1, 2015, which has its primary listening base in the Twin Falls, Idaho area. I was told and shown about Steve before I met him, as well the others I interviewed with. I believe the real purpose of that interview has not yet been seen.

Lastly, I appeared on the Bryan Hyde radio talk show twice following my 18-month speaking mission. Those were unplanned events, meaning, I had thought I was finished with radio interviews, but when we talked about doing a show together we both felt it would be a good idea. It was on Bryan's show that I made the more formal announcement of the Wasatch Wakeup. All in all, the radio shows were a worthwhile way of getting the word out about my story. Those shows are still available on my website.

Public Speaking Events

Each of the radio shows took place intermittently throughout the eighteen-month publicity portion of my mission. In addition to radio air time, I spoke at over 22 events. Each speaking event was unique, but there were a number of elements that were common among them. As a general rule, I would be contacted by a willing volunteer host acting under the direction of the spirit, who would find a meeting location and invite the attendees.

In most cases, I didn't even know the hosts, but they were so kind and would often personally fund reservation fees, provide room and board, as well as meals, and in many cases they even paid for my flight getting to the speaking event. Throughout my time among them they would pick me up and drop me off at the airport, and drive me around between events. The success of this portion of the mission was due in large part to the wonderful hosts who had followed the promptings they had received and sacrificed so much to make them possible.

I was instructed by the spirit that my speaking events needed to primarily focus on testifying of Jesus Christ and his Mission, and the reality of the Plan of Salvation. I spent very little time dwelling on my near-death experiences and future calamities in comparison to testifying of Christ. I understood that the words would be given to me in the hour that I would need them—a form of revelation I often refer to as a "live feed."

While I was formally responsible for the speaking events, my hosts handled most of the details. My only involvement for the most part was to approve what they had planned, such as the locations, times, number of attendees, and mode of inviting them.

One of the most joyful experiences for me throughout that portion of my mission was to see myself in vision at a future speaking event, and within weeks I would be contacted by someone asking me if they could host that event. It was a continual witness to me that I was not the orchestrator of the mission, and that the Lord truly was in the details.

Some events went smoothly and without incident, and others were surrounded by more dramatic events and will require more description to cover some important details than others. Each event is outlined chronologically as follows:

Kaysville, Utah
July 15, 2014

The Kaysville event was coordinated by Kerri and Crystal. They chose to take a "by invite only" approach, and contacted about 115 people from an emergency preparedness group. They hosted it with a luncheon at a church building there in Kaysville. My publisher Chad and a good friend from college were in attendance at the event, adding some comfort and familiarity.

As my first speaking engagement, that event took a lot of courage, and the spirit was very strong, causing a lot of emotion. The audience was very kind and respectful. I could not have asked for a better first time speaking event to ease me into that phase of my mission. I let everyone know it was my first time, so they went easy on me.

It was a relatively small gathering, but large enough to make me feel the seriousness of what I was getting involved in. I consider myself to be someone who values privacy, so to suddenly be in the spotlight and the subject of everyone's attention was overwhelming. While I'm far from a celebrity, I did learn what that lifestyle is like to an extent.

For example, I learned that if I needed to use the restroom, it would be a good idea to have someone guard it, otherwise I might be cornered and approached for photo opportunities, or autographs. I wasn't abused in any way at the Kaysville event, but the spirit helped me to understand that precaution and security would be needful moving forward.

It was as though the spirit coordinated that occasion to be a safe setting of mostly friendly people with sincere interests in attendance to ease me into what would eventually become more hostile. In fact, it might be likened to a missionary training center experience, sort of preparing me for the mission field in a controlled atmosphere. The majority of those in attendance at that meeting are still friendly to me to this day.

Logan Tabernacle
July 17, 2014

Logan is one of the older Mormon settlements in the Rocky Mountains, and its early settlers built a beautiful tabernacle there. In the last century it was turned over to the city of Logan as a public meeting hall. It seats 2,000 people, and so it made a great meeting place for my second speaking event.

I had seen this event in vision prior to speaking, and knew it would be in the Logan Tabernacle. I had seen the number of people in attendance would be about 500. I sensed the presence of many from the other side of the veil and was told there were about 5,000 of them in attendance. Due to the rich Mormon pioneer history of the area I knew many of the heavenly visitors were pioneers and early settlers to the valley. I also discerned the presence of some founding fathers, Book of Mormon figures like Moroni and many of Helaman's Stripling Warriors, and spirits guarding the building. Some were people from the City of Enoch.

I sensed spiritual warfare going on outside the Tabernacle. The adversary had a number of hosts with intentions to thwart the message I had to share, but those from the light side were there to keep them at bay. There were so many angelic protectors on the stage with me that the stage felt crowded, even to the point that it affected me physically and I felt like I was being pushed back, even though there was only me and a few seated on the bench behind me.

Those in mortal attendance were a mixed crowd. As I gazed across the audience I discerned some evil entities with attachments to some of the crowd members. I sensed some with pornography addictions, and women living in abusive situations, which were conditions I sensed at every speaking event. I tried my best to focus on the Lord's love and the message I was there to deliver. Also in attendance were translated and resurrected beings, which the spirit helped me to discern.

It quickly became evident to me the great interest in my message on both sides of the veil, both from light and dark beings. While there were empty seats in the tabernacle that day by most accounts, a few other people with the gift of sight later told me in person or by email that they saw a full house. It was a testimony to me that the Lord cared about this speaking mission, that it was inspired of him, and that he wanted the message to get out.

South Jordan, Utah
July 20, 2014

A woman named Emily living in South Jordan hosted this event at her home, with about 110 people in attendance. It was a beautiful home with vaulted ceilings, which were filled with heavenly attendees. I was also forewarned that this event may produce some skeptics and hecklers. I was grateful for this warning. Following the traditional speaking format of bearing testimony of the Savior and the plan, I entertained some questions, and recalled a man asking the question, "How can you know the difference between revelation and your own mind?" It was a question I identified with, having asked it frequently myself.

Mesa, Arizona
August 23, 2014

As Mesa was only a two-hour drive from my home in Oro Valley, I decided to go by car, leaving Jeff and the kid's home that Saturday night. As usual, I had received some foresight on generally how the event would go, and about the size of the crowd. On that occasion, I discerned that the event would get a late start. My gracious host was running a little behind that night, leaving some of the early patrons a little anxious and slightly irritated the building hadn't been opened and chairs hadn't been placed.

I arrived 45 minutes before the meeting, and drove around the event location to discern the energy of the forming crowd. I parked my car and as soon as I stepped out, was met by a group of about 35 people. Crowd management became a necessity, and was concerning to me at times. Simple tasks like using the restroom presented challenges with well-meaning people who sought photo opportunities and isolated conversations. I had been cautioned about crowds and usually had a number of priesthood holders to offer some protection, but hadn't done so on that occasion. It reinforced the need to do so at future speaking events.

I enjoyed a visit with the crowd outside for 30 minutes or so before going in the building, and then spoke casually for another hour or so as chairs were set up and I awaited the more formal meeting. The building was more than adequately sized with a seating potential of around 600, which ultimately had three to four hundred people in attendance.

I had been warned for several months by the spirit that my speaking events were not to be affiliated in any way with the LDS church, unless my hosts had worked through proper priesthood channels, which did happen on a few of the events. I learned that just prior to the Mesa event a well-meaning person distributed flyers announcing that Julie Rowe would be speaking that night to the general public and placed those flyers in the car windshields of patrons of the Mesa Arizona LDS Temple.

That effort produced about 30 people at my event who were unfamiliar with my message. The flyers went against the instruction I had received and given, and created a problem. Firstly, my approach was to have invitations given by word of mouth, trusting that a more welcoming and like-minded audience would participate. Secondly, I knew protocol with regard to the LDS Church was important, and knew that policy had been breached.

By that time in the public speaking portion of my mission. I had sold 8,000 copies of my books, and was still widely unknown in the church, let alone the world. Following the event, a number of individuals who had been blindsided by this strange, unknown visionary woman petitioned church headquarters concerning me, and whether I was even a member of the church, if I was in good standing, and so forth.

I knew by the spirit that most or all of the apostles had received inquiries, but knew they were more common among Elder Ballard and Elder Oaks' offices. A few weeks later I was called in to my Stake President's office for questioning.

The speaking event began and flowed like my other events, but with quite a number of individuals unfamiliar with my story, it produced a few hecklers. One man who had apparently just walked in off the street asked in a perturbed tone, "Help me understand how anything you have to say has any relevance to my life."

In the 30 seconds or so that the man's apparent irritations and attack more than question surfaced, I understood that the man struggled with pornography, that his wife had left him, and they were going through custody issues over their children.

I sensed an- audible gasp from the audience from the abruptness of his tone, but then sensing the more serious part of his question, I said in effect: "Sir, help me understand. Are you currently in a relationship right now. Are you married?"

He answered, "No, I'm going through a divorce."

I then replied, "That's my understanding. Sir, this can help you a great deal. If you love your children, and you listen to this message and prepare them for the future, this will help them. If you don't listen, you're right, I can't help you."

I felt that he was chastened by the spirit, sat down, and then left the meeting hall within about five minutes. Some people emailed me following the event expressing their admiration for the way I respectfully handled the man's spirited energy.

Following the event, my Stake President told me many people had been calling church headquarters. Rumors had started circulating that perhaps I had been disfellowshipped or excommunicated, so some had tracked down where I lived in Arizona, and tracked down my stake, and then contacted him to learn something of my status in the church.

Someone reported that I sold books at that speaking event. I had to defend the situation, explaining that permission had been given from the stake president where the meeting was held, and that it was not an actual stake building, but was a facility where they conducted plays, and even rented it out for other venues. I had also been given permission to sell books, which included one box of 40. Seagull Book, who carried my books at the time, was just down the road, so I didn't think it necessary to bring more than that.

The real concern was that if the church had permitted the selling of books on church property, it could have threatened the church's tax exempt status, which is ultimately why I was called in. My Stake President read from the handbook, and then told me, "If you were in my jurisdiction I would not have you speak again." I was sure that I hadn't done anything wrong, but sensed more of his distaste for my near-death experience, rather than anything to do with the church.

Another agitated man in an accusatory tone said before the crowd, "You said on the Radio with Mills Crenshaw that President Monson is the one who would issue the call to gather to camps."

I quickly cut him off and replied in effect, "Sir, I'm sorry but you have misunderstood. I have never said it was President Monson."

He argued back and insisted two to three times that he knew I had said it, as he accused me of lying and back peddling. I then said, "Sir, I know who the prophet is, but there are certain topics that are off limits for me to state publicly, and I can tell you that I know I have never said that on the radio or in any public setting that he is the one to issue the call."

The man still wouldn't back down, but the spirit guided me to redirect the meeting and things continued relatively smoothly after that.

Three weeks later, I received an email from the man who had by that time revisited the radio talk show audio files published on my website, and he apologized. He had re-listened to every interview and realized that I had never stated nor implied who would issue a call to gather.

Chicago, Illinois
September 26-27, 2014

I flew to the Chicago area on September 25, 2014. I didn't do any sightseeing other than driving through the city and attending the Chicago Temple on that trip, and really didn't on any of my speaking trips. On the next day I was scheduled to speak, an off-site air traffic control center caught on fire, which led to the redirecting of air traffic and created a delay for a number of people who would attend the event in the region. Some would miss it completely.

The local news report of the event was that a disgruntled employee had set fire to the building. I had been given foresight of that event and had seen the bigger picture; that foul-play was involved and a murder had occurred there. I was also told to fly in on the day before the speaking event, which if I hadn't listened to, I would have missed it. Flying or driving to my destination a day early became a common practice for the remainder of the speaking events.

My travel expenses on that trip were covered by my Saturday host, who also provided lodging for me during my time in the Chicago area. Additionally she drove me to the Chicago suburb of Aurora where I would speak at a residence on a Friday night before thirty to forty people who had been gathered. My hosts were very kind, but I regretted needing to leave soon after the event and not getting to spend any time with them.

The next night took place at my host's high-rise residence in Chicago, near the Willis Tower and overlooking the lake and the park. My host from the previous night came again, and as I addressed my new audience I thanked both hosts for having me. My first host began crying and spoke up and let me know before the audience that she was disappointed to not have had more time with her. She had prayed her whole life to have a near-death experience or to meet someone who had so she could learn more of the spirit world. When I had come and gone in a flash, and she had no opportunity to engage in discussion with me, she was discouraged.

There were about 20 participants that afternoon and we were welcomed with a nice luncheon. I spoke for an hour and a-half, giving the same Christ-centered message I had done at other events, and then opened it up to some questions. I had to tread lightly on some of the questions concerning future events in Chicago, of all places, one of the more sobering scenes I have observed in vision and we were right in the middle of it. Discussing the tower that would be blown up, the museum that would catch fire, the protests and riots in the streets which were all within view would have invoked fear, which was not in any way part of my message. Some of those who attended drove from great distances to hear me, including Missouri and Maryland.

The atmosphere was casual and warming as individuals bonded well with each other. Some individuals from that group will become very key individuals in the future of relief. I felt that if for no other reason in going to Chicago, meeting those people was worth it. A photograph was taken at the event that showed peculiar orbs of light, which some later read into as angelic beings. When word of that got on the internet, it created a small stir and created more skeptics and antagonists.

The spiritual opposition in that city was strong on that trip for a number of reasons; but I was prepared for and protected at that event. I discerned some warriors from Helaman's armies were there in a protecting capacity, in addition to some of my ancestors. I believed that if they had not been there I would have had an adversarial attack.

Springville, Utah
November 7, 2014

In November of 2014 I flew to Utah from Iowa. It was a book signing event rather than a speaking event, and was hosted at the Springville Community Center by Chad, the publisher of my books. His wife and daughters helped sell books, while Chad and his sons acted as security.

There were over 800 people in attendance and I signed around 500 books. I spoke to the crowd, but because it was primarily a book signing, I condensed my usual message down to about 25 minutes. Chad, who is also spiritually gifted, saw a number of attending spirits both of the light and dark sort.

It was the first time I had seen a particular family in person that I had seen in vision. About a year following that event, the father in the family approached me and I learned that he was a very spiritually gifted person who came to see for himself if I was legit. He shared his witness that he had seen several people guarding me from the other side, and in particular a large angel who he saw with his eyes. He let me know that it raised a question in his mind, which he mentally asked of the Lord. The question was, "Who is she, what has she done, or what will she do that would warrant the need for those heavenly protectors?"

I came to recognize that his son, who is nine years younger than me, was the young man who had appeared to me in spirit when I was a young girl in Hawaii, and was frightened at the scene of an ancient child sacrifice location.

This event was the last time I would announce a large scale book signing open to the public. Chad wrote the following letter to a woman who later wanted to host a book signing, in which he explained why they couldn't host another book signing event. It also breaks down the ratios of the different kinds of attendees at the Logan and Springville events:

"The main reason for our extreme caution is because of Julie's past experiences at book signings. At her first event in Logan, we had about 500 people at the book signing. I would say about 300 were fully supportive, 175 were curiosity seekers, and 25 were clearly there to oppose her.

"Two months later, we held a similar event in Springville, and we had about 800 people. It was now 600 supporters, 100 curiosity seekers, and 100 true enemies, several of whom got confrontational with Julie. Some of these enemies had traveled hundreds of miles to be there. It was a bit scary and it felt like we were on the verge of violence. I was within seconds of grabbing one guy and dragging him out. I know we had heavenly aid to keep them at bay. At that point we quit doing book signings, mainly for Julie's safety."

Seattle, Washington
September 27, 2014

Dawn of Seattle and Jon, who had just moved to Idaho from Seattle, hosted this event. Dawn graciously covered our travel costs, provided meals and a bed for me, and went through considerable effort to secure a meeting place, which was at an LDS Stake Center. Hosting such a non-church affiliated event at a church building can be a lot of work.

Dawn later recalled in an email message: *"I had many hurdles to overcome in getting Julie to Seattle, and in getting permission to use our chapel after other venues failed. It was these odd events that miraculously and unconventionally resolved themselves that witnessed to me that I was getting help from beyond the veil in this process of bringing Julie to Seattle to share her message. God was involved and this was a good thing to do in spite of opposition from many people near and dear to me. I put my reputation on the line with my adult children and local priesthood leaders in making this event happen. It was hard, and it was important."*

Two nights before I began my journey west, I was prompted to grab a few extra books and was told I would have the chance to give those away. I had the privilege of staying at the Kansas City Temple president and his wife's home in Iowa, who had another guest as well, who I knew should receive the extra book. That guest would later become an important member of the Greater Tomorrow Relief Fund.

I then flew to Seattle and was able to attend the Seattle Temple with my hosts, and I had a good experience there. The weather that day was not surprisingly partly cloudy with light rain. Prior to speaking I had received a priesthood blessing, which helped settle my nerves and invited the spirit. Interestingly, when Jon gave me the blessing, he stated my full name without asking me, which surprised me, since I hadn't told him my middle name. This was evidence to me that Jon lived by the spirit, and again that the Lord was involved in these speaking events.

About 300 guests were seated ten minutes before the meeting began. Some hymns were sung, and an opening prayer was given. I was introduced by my host and then I began my usual speech testifying of the Lord's plan, and having faith and trusting in Him. Despite the blessing I had received, I still had some health issues that drained my energy. I sensed two heavenly helpers bracing me during the event, and I later had witnesses of that. I recalled witnessing the same thing during President Monson's General Conference address the following April when his strength failed him, and angelic beings supported him. This served as an additional witness to me of the important nature of this speaking event.

At some point during the speech I used a metaphor of dragons with regard to the adversaries' influence in our lives, in what I often call spiritual warfare. This later caused a little stir on the internet in efforts to make me appear misguided and delusional, which I found odd, since I was using the same imagery that had been used by John in the Book of Revelation.

My host later said of the event, *"From my many conversations with her I was impressed with her intense desire to please God, and to do nothing to offend His prophets and priesthood leaders; that seemed to be uppermost in her mind and it put my heart at ease. I felt she knew her experiences were real and from God and she was willing to be persecuted in the process of sharing her knowledge and experience. I felt she was not after fame, fortune or attention. She did what she did out of love for God and other people's well being."*

Texas
February 5-7, 2015

My Texas trip was coordinated and hosted by a man named Dan Exby and his wife Courtney. Dan's father Jim was my Bishop back when I lived in Kansas, and Dan was kind enough to donate frequent flyer miles to aid in my travel.

Had things gone my way, I would have stayed at hotels during my speaking events, for the peace and quiet they would provide me from the emotional experiences that would precede and follow speaking. But the spirit always directed me to stay with individuals, who had dedicated homes, and where I would find another form of rest—the kind I had been coming to recognize that comes through service.

My hosts had three children under the age of six. At that time their three-year old and toddler were having nightmares in the middle of the night which caused them to lose sleep. Since I was staying at their home I was able to do some energy work on the children. Between their prayers and mine, they reported a short time later that their children had started sleeping through the night, which was a blessing for them.

Dan had some friends who had come in from California and Pennsylvania to attend the event. The original plan was to hold the speaking event at the host's residence, but due to the number of attendees it had been changed to a church building, which was the way I had always seen it before the event. I made important contacts during that trip that would play an important role down the road.

Cameron, Missouri
February 21, 2015

Since it was only a short drive away, Jeff and our children accompanied me, and it was the first time Jeff had heard my message delivered in a public setting in person, and was the second time for the kids who heard me speak in Logan. There were a mixture of attendees from Kansas, Missouri, Illinois, and Iowa, totaling about 350 people in attendance on this side of the veil.

The meeting began by singing all four verses from the hymn, "I Know That My Redeemer Lives." During the first measure of the song I recognized heavenly choirs singing with us. One of the more notable experiences from that event came following, when a couple people additionally witnessed the enhanced sound of angelic choirs.

I was touched to hear that even my husband Jeff and our children detected the heavenly sounding music. Each of my children have manifest spiritual gifts at times of their lives, but coming from Jeff was quite surprising. A number of others randomly emailed me following the event to add their witness to hearing heavenly music. One of those people had led the music during the St. Louis temple dedication and let me know that was the only other time she had heard heavenly music.

Of that experience, one attendee submitted the following account on December 31, 2016:

I was there in Cameron Missouri and would like to share my observations. The opening hymn in Cameron Missouri was "I Know That My Redeemer Lives." When we all stood and sang to open the meeting, I had a curious awareness of the quality of sound that group of people made. It was nothing like I've heard at church, or at stake conference, even while at General Conference. The quality of sound I heard far exceeded the aggregate talent of those in that room, it got my attention, I did not want it to stop. I thought to myself why aren't we singing another hymn. It hadn't even crossed my mind that angelic beings may have been there. Shows just how little I knew at the time.

To this day, I can hear that beautiful choir in my head - it was something that made a permanent imprint on my soul. And how appropriate for such a pure group of people only wanting to know what it is the Lord would have them do to bring to pass his great plan.

I have often looked back at that experience and wondered why the veil had been so thin, even more so than at other events. I am still working on finding an answer to that, but in hindsight I learned that the Lord gave me an indication at each one of the speaking events that He was aware of the events. I took it to be a symbol of his acceptance and gladness at the way I was conducting my mission. I delivered my message of the Savior in the usual manner and it turned out to be a really good experience.

St. George, Utah
March 7, 2015

My host was a woman named Pam, a resident of southern Utah, and who was helped quite a bit by her daughter Emily. Pam was kind enough to cover my flight to Utah, and provided sleeping accommodations at her home, in addition to picking me up and dropping me off from the airport, and providing meals. She was a wonderful host!

The speaking event took place in the Dixie Convention Center, with about 1,200 people in attendance, 150 or so of which were translated beings. Many of those attendees came from the Las Vegas area, and a good number from parts of Arizona, in addition to residents of St. George. The cost to rent the facility was $1,100 and was covered by my hosts.

The Convention Center had become available only two days before the event. Pam had originally reserved a church building in Las Vegas, and then the St. George Tabernacle, but neither of those facilities could have accommodated the large crowd, which was so tight that many had to sit on the ground and I could hardly walk through them.

I sensed about 60,000 from the other side of veil also in attendance, which included those with dark and light intentions. Among the purer side I discerned some of the ancient New Testament apostles, some of the Founding Fathers, early LDS prophets, and many pioneers from early days of the church. Of all my speaking events, St. George for whatever reason produced the most impressive attendance from the other side of the veil.

The presence of such spiritual attendees seemed to always be the case at large gatherings, though fewer in number. It was as though the adversary did not like me addressing that many people, and so I had a sense of the spiritual warfare that was going on among light and dark spirits in the other realm.

I covered the same speaking agenda as with other events,

focusing on my witness of the Savior and the plan. I spoke about repentance, and spoke less about my near-death experience, and less about future events in that region than I had done at any other speaking event because of the mixed crowd. I sensed some of the attendees had come with ulterior motives to discredit or to mock me.

I knew the majority of the audience wanted to hear specific future visionary experiences I had for their region, essentially there as sign seekers. I felt that I and the audience were given the understanding that such would not be the case, and that I was not a soothsayer there to predict their future, but was there to testify of Christ.

After 45 minutes of sharing my testimony, I was impressed to speak in an unusual way, addressing groups of individuals with similar spiritual needs and questions. I would begin a sentence customized by the spirit to their needs, and then before finishing the sentence would begin another sentence addressing another group, and repeated that process a few times. The idea was that those who were in tune would have the sentence completed for them by the power of the Holy Ghost.

The effect worked for some, but created confusion in many, assuming that I had an incomplete train of thought, or that I was all over the map. I knew while I was doing it that I would be criticized by those who were confused, and so I was.

I really got the audience's attention when I said in effect, "Some of you are wondering why I'm here, what this is all about, and may be wondering when are we going to get to the good stuff?" I then said, "So, let's talk."

Then I heard an audible sigh across the room, some yelling "Yeah," and then about 300 people leaned forward in their seats, ready to hear something exciting. I said, "That's not why I'm here."

I felt the energy shift, and immediately felt negative emotions come from many of them as if to say "We came all this way, and now we're not going to hear the good stuff."

When I left I was thronged by the crowd, and many passed me by and gave glaring looks. I began to see that large speaking events had their disadvantages. I noticed a number of elderly and physically handicapped people among the crowd who were unable to find a seat. I was a little disappointed to see that those who had fought for their well-positioned seats wouldn't share with those who had greater needs than their own. I knew some of those special needs individuals were actually translated beings offering a test to some of those saints.

Gifts of the spirit were manifest at the St. George event. One of the attendees submitted the following witness:

The day before the event, I drove uptown to purchase something small at the hardware store. When I exited my vehicle, my nose caught the scent of a pleasant men's cologne. I looked around, but no men were nearby, and I sniffed the hedges to see if they were the source of the smell, but they were not. I stopped at customer service to ask directions to find my item, but there was a line.

Before I decided to get out of the line, I smelled another, distinctly different pleasant men's cologne. I turned to the man behind me to compliment him on the scent, but he was homeless looking, and obviously not the source of the smell, so I stayed quiet. Then, as I was looking at the selection of items on the aisle, I smelled another, different pleasant men's cologne. I looked up and down the aisle, but no one was around. After making my purchase, I walked out to my vehicle and I remember asking myself aloud, "Why am I smelling all these smells?"

About halfway through the event, Julie Rowe paused slightly and said something about not knowing why, but she mentioned those who were "smelling smells." My mind immediately went to my experience at the hardware store, and I knew it was a spiritual confirmation meant for me. I did not have a feeling that Julie is a prophet, psychic, or other type of leader, but I knew the message for me was, "The time is now to prepare for a greater tomorrow."

I have since had a heightened awareness of scents and smells, believing that I now recognize a spiritual gift I had never before heard of! My nose is newly sensitive to all types of smells. My family has accepted the scenario of a callout, and we have prepared and practiced all aspects in order to be prepared to go when called.

As with other speaking events, a side benefit of speaking was that it had a natural way of getting key individuals in contact with me who would later contribute to the overall rescue effort.

Fayetteville, Tennessee
April 10, 2015

I stayed with my very gracious hosts in Tennessee. The husband was not on board with my message, but was very kind and respectful. I gathered that they were surprised that I would go to what felt like the middle of nowhere Tennessee, but I came to see that the Lord was sending a message that he loves all of his children regardless of where they live or their circumstances.

More than 80 people were in attendance at the county courthouse, which presented an interesting energy dynamic for me. I followed the same speaking format of other events and things went smoothly. Following the event, a woman came up to me who had the gift of discerning of spirits, and saw a woman off to my left who was whispering the words that I would speak, and there was a huge man off to my right acting in a protective capacity.

Boston, Massachusetts
May 8-11, 2015

During my trip to Boston, I was delighted but not surprised that a number of the founding fathers were in attendance, including George Washington, James Madison, and John

Adams, as well as Moroni from the Book of Mormon, and others. I knew of their presence, not with my physical senses, but the spiritual.

Only rarely did I ever see spirits with my physical eyes, so I was always grateful for an additional witness at my speaking events. Two of the eleven or so attendees let me know following the event that they had discerned them as well. I knew their sincerity when one of them pointed to the exact location that I had seen George Washington standing.

Burke, Virginia
June 6, 2015

My Virginia host was named Tammy. She picked me up and made arrangements for me to stay with her parents across the street. When I met her mother who had cancer, I had the impression of how much longer she would live, and could see where the cancer was located in her body. I felt one of the main reasons I spoke at that event was to meet Tammy's family, which I feel a strong connection to. Tammy's mother later passed away from cancer.

Meeting them created a connection for me to later speak in Denver at Tammy's sister's house. An attendee who I had gotten to know a little better from the Chicago event was in attendance, and I was prompted to ask him to stand and introduce me. I met one of my cousins while on that trip as well, which added some depth to the visit.

During the event, someone asked me if I had talked to Glenn Beck, to which I replied that I hadn't—yet. Some people caught on to that remark and put it on the internet, which created another little stir and some antagonists.

Annapolis, Maryland
June 7, 2015

This event was very similar to the night before. Participants were there by invite only and totaled about 40. I was told to have a new friend named Brandon speak and introduce me to the group. I was privileged to meet a distant cousin, which made the event memorable as well. Many of the individuals in attendance at this event are now part of GTRF, and will become regional contacts, which was another key purpose in gathering at this event.

Utah
June 19-22, 2015

I had two speaking events in June of 2015 which were close enough to each other that I made a single trip out of it. The first event took place at Mount Pleasant on June 19. The event participants were by invitation only, which was according to the direction I had received.

A man named Steve was the host and was kind enough to fly me and my family out to Utah, and treated us to a four wheel ride in the mountains overlooking the Sanpete Valley while staying there. It was the closest I was able to get to a bird's eye view of events I had seen in vision in that would take place there, and I knew there was a higher purpose in the 4-wheel ride.

The speaking event was an informal get together at Steve's home. He had invited a number of his family members and I regretted telling him that they couldn't come as I had been directed who would be there. There were about 15 people in attendance, many of which would play important roles in my relief organization later on.

While there I sensed the presence of Captain Moroni's army as my spiritual protection throughout the trip. Ray Lambert, who would later be a radio host for me, was in attendance at the event with his wife. I had the sense that his wife would soon pass on, which happened six months later, and it caused me some heartfelt emotion at the event.

Weber State University
Ogden, Utah
June 22, 2015

I began having visuals and dreams of the Ogden speaking event in the Fall of 2014. I was shown that it would be a trying experience, and that messengers both on the light and dark sides would be present, and that the adversary had clear intentions of harassing me.

Feeling concern, I sought confirmation of the conditions of the event from my publisher Chad, and asked his advice on whether I ought to attend or not. He also sensed the impending trouble, but he agreed that despite the difficulty it would be an important event in my speaking mission.

The event was held at Weber State University in conjunction with another well-attended conference. Of that experience, one attendee later commented: *"I could see forms of angelic beings surrounding the stage and guarding the stairs up to the stage. I also saw two giant forms of angels on either side of her on the stage. They were massive and very tall. I got the feeling that they had a purpose in protection from those that would do harm from both sides of the veil. I haven't had an experience like that before or since where I could see forms of angelic beings. It was amazing."*

Colorado
July 5-7, 2015

Five months previous to my Colorado trip, my brother got word that I would be coming later in the year to speak in Colorado where he and my siblings lived. By that time my books had come out, which created a stir and some embarrassment for my family. Through the course of the phone call my brother's tactic evolved from a feigned interest in caring for me, to saying my health issues should keep me home, to threats saying I wasn't to come to Colorado. He said I was crazy, that my siblings had all tried to ignore this Julie Rowe embarrassment, and if I came to his backyard it wouldn't end well for our family.

A woman named Sarah helped to coordinate my first event in Castle Rock, and was kind enough to pay for my flight. I flew into Denver from Iowa on July 5th, and spoke that night at the home of Becky, my host. It was a large home that accommodated about 130 people.

Becky coordinated that event in a general public invitation by registration format, so attendees were essentially screened. The general public registration created a diverse audience. A number of attendees were there seeking answers and clarity of who I was and if I was genuine or not. One man had come to Utah from Australia and made the drive to Colorado to hear me speak. Additionally, I received two threatening emails a couple weeks before the event.

Three days before I received a bizarre email from a woman who said she and her "soul twin" would be in attendance, and that they were instructed by her "master" to identify herself at the event, and a number of other strange comments. I had understood from the spirit that she was possessed and had been given a visual of the event.

It was a strange experience, but I came to understand that the adversary was using this woman to intimidate me, incite fear, and let me know that the adversary was aware of me and my mission. I was also shown that the woman was actually part of a satanic cult. When I saw her and her "soul twin" who had actually turned out to be a man, I discerned two inch horns on the man's head with my spiritual eyes. It was very strange.

Following the meeting, my security team of about 12 people

got nervous as they each watched the woman go up and give me a hug. They knew without being told that she was the one to watch for.

Half of my siblings came to hear me speak, while the other half went to a cabin two hours away from Denver for the weekend, leaving the day I arrived and returning just the day before I left.

The second speaking event took place in Fort Collins at a school auditorium two days later on July 7th. The auditorium had a seating capacity of around 1,000 but ultimately seated about 330 people. To my spiritual eyes, every seat was filled, and we had a full house that night. Before speaking I was treated to lunch by my hosts, the Wilkes. They personally funded the rental of the auditorium and some other expenses, and were very kind.

That event had a stark contrast to the event two nights previously. The hymns were powerful, there were no naysayers there to impede the spirit, and with the Ogden and Denver negative events behind me, it created an amazing and spiritual event that I thoroughly enjoyed. Like other events, I had seen myself in the facility, but it was always really cool for me to get the confirmation of the location and even many of the audience members in person that validated my foresight.

Rexburg, Idaho
July 25, 2015

The Rexburg speaking event was surreal for me. I had known for eight months that it would mark the end of my speaking mission. I had a sense of the people who would be in attendance, which would include some of the Founding Fathers and Pioneers with roots and a heritage in the Rexburg area. I even had a sense of some of the mortals who would attend, and some of my past and future interactions with them. I also knew some members of my husband's distant family would be there.

The event was announced in May, and plans began to unfold. I delegated all the preparations for the event to a woman named Tonya. As with all the other speaking venues, I stayed out of the planning details, but asked that this event not take place in an LDS facility. Participants were invited from the public but tickets needed to be requested in order to attend.

Tickets had sold out after the first day. I suspected part of the reason was that many people had reserved a high number of tickets for family and friends, and therefore asked Tonya to find a way to be more specific with tickets. It was decided that individuals would need to reserve tickets once again, but for themselves only. Approximately 900 registrants were contacted individually by Tonya and her helpers by email to explain what happened and how to proceed registering for more tickets. I had also asked Tonya to reserve the first three rows for family and other attendees.

The meeting was preceded by a number of congregational hymns directed by a woman named Angela. One man reported: *"To this day I don't think I've ever felt the spirit so strong during singing as I felt that night. As I've considered why this might be, I have concluded that it was because I was gathered with hundreds of other like minded individuals, who were eager to learn more, and were largely one in purpose. Anyway, I was deeply touched to the point that I could not vocalize the words of the hymns on many occasions."*

Before I appeared on stage I had been crying, which some from the audience especially on the front rows noticed. I was emotional from the familiarity of the place, the people, and was also very moved by the intense feelings of the spirit during the hymns. For the next hour I delivered my witness of the Savior, his mission, and some of my experiences in the church and some of my gospel insights.

Then sensing the humble and open nature of the audience, I turned the balance of the time over to a question answer session. My mood switched as I began to anticipate the questions and tried to lighten things up. For the next hour I felt a range of emotions including laughter, sorrow, and deep emotions as I discussed some future events.

As the evening drew to a close, I answered what was anticipated to be the last question and then I asked for a moment to consider if I had covered everything. Just then I received an impression that a certain question had not been asked by a woman on my left, about ten rows back. I looked in her direction as the words of her question came to mind concerning the ability of nutrition to play a role in bringing health to people.

Following the event, I looked through the remaining questions written on paper scraps and found the question the woman wanted to ask. Weeks later that woman took the time to email me and let me know how touching it was for her.

The meeting concluded as the congregation sang Redeemer of Israel. One of the participants from the audience shared her experience with that closing hymn: "*It felt as though there were Pioneers singing with us. It was loud/strong but reverent and beautiful. Julie was emotional. I was emotional, as well as many other people.*"

Part of the emotion I felt was from the great spirit of the hymn and that meeting overall, but it was also in knowing I had just completed a monumental portion of my speaking mission, and it was time for me to rest—but only for a short time.

With the public speaking portion of my mission behind me, I reflected on the entire experience and realized it coincided with the traditional female LDS sister mission of eighteen months. It was the sort of 'coincidence' that was too common to be truly coincidental, considering it to be a tender mercy of the Lord.

Over the course of my eighteen month mission I flew over

28,000 miles, addressed over 7,200 people, visited 12 U.S. states, gave around 400 books at my own cost, and spent around 60 days away from my family. Jeff and I spent a significant amount of our personal funds in order to testify of the Savior and create a greater awareness of things to come.

I received personal attacks and death threats for telling my story to the world. Some were bold enough to make accusations of my personal character and would say to my face that I was "a pawn of the devil," or that I was evil. Adding insult to injury, every one of those attacks came from members of my faith. I didn't receive a single threat or unkind remark from someone outside of my faith.

An added hardship of being in the public eye came through my interactions with various kinds of people. I learned through sad experience that there are those who would use me for my 'celebrity status', got what they wanted and dropped me like a hotcake. Others I found to be energy leeches, and I had to part with them to be able to move forward. Others wanted me to tell them their future, etc.

Along the way I had to learn to discern true friends, from those that would use me. I learned that others only listened to me as some sort of "freak show." I often made people angry because I didn't provide the nitty-gritty details they wanted, but rather focused on trust in the Lord, His mission, and having faith. I also found through those events that there are many true and pure people who follow the Lord, and followed me for the right reasons, and I am very grateful for the many wonderful contacts and friends I made throughout the public speaking mission; many of the purposes of which are yet to be realized.

Whether people believe my story or not, to speak of my entire 18-month mission's hardships and expenses as a whole is a witness in itself of my conviction of the message I was directed to share. But if success can be measured by the number of people that were reached and whose hearts were touched, and who were more motivated to focus their efforts on spiritual and physical preparedness, then my mission was successful.

CHAPTER ELEVEN

The Greater Tomorrow
Relief Fund

With my speaking mission behind me I began to return to life as I knew it, less in the public spotlight; but a new mission was in the process of emerging. Over the previous eighteen months I had met hundreds of people across the country with varying interests, skills, and eagerness to help and contribute to a humanitarian effort I knew I would begin at some point in the future. I was eager to establish an organization that would provide relief to those in need in years to come, and soon found out the adversary wanted to stop that from happening.

On August 31, 2015, I was taking my daughter to volleyball practice when I was contacted by a KUTV news reporter based in Utah. The reporter was seeking a statement from me concerning a leaked internal memo from the Church Seminary and Institutes department of The Church of Jesus Christ of Latter-day Saints, entitled "Spurious Materials in Circulation."

This memo is updated periodically to clarify statements given by General Authorities, halt circulating rumors within the Church, or lists books that are used by teachers inappropriately in the classroom. I knew a media storm was coming for several months at that time and wasn't overly concerned, so I directed the request to my husband and Chad, who had become my press liaison, so I could drop my daughter off. My husband wrote the following response for me:

"I agree that the curriculum for LDS church classes should only come from sources recognized by the LDS Church as being authoritative. My story is not intended to be authoritative nor to create any church doctrine. It is simply part of my personal journey that I have chosen to share in hopes that it can help people to prepare for the times we live in by increasing their faith in Christ and by looking to our prophet and church leaders for guidance."

Chad made the following statement to the press: *"Julie and I wholeheartedly agree with the Church's stance that these accounts should not be shared in seminary or institute classes."*

The story of the leaked memo spread from one news station to another, and within a week had made headlines worldwide. Adding fuel to the flame, a significant lunar eclipse was only weeks away and some clever reporters capitalized on the opportunity to make me appear to be a crazy "end of the world" freak show. Anti-Mormon groups loved the negative light I had been put in, and fabricated their own stories targeting my message, which was to follow the Savior Jesus Christ and heed the living prophet.

My email exploded with activity from both supporters and haters, which included a range of activity from name calling and silly accusations, to very real threats on me and my families' lives. I compiled a document that included over sixty names I had been called by many members of my church, and others around the world.

I was told by more than three people that I was a "pawn of the devil." I was told by another that I was an "awful person" and that I had "ruined" their life. Others felt I should know what an awful mother and terrible wife I was, and that I was "the worst thing to happen to this world."

The most notable threat came through the disguise of an email from someone who had feigned friendship toward me. In it they explained that they believed me story, and then invited me to go and attend a conference at one of two five-star hotels in Saudi Arabia or Switzerland, where I would explain to them everything that I had seen in vision concerning those two locations' past, present, and future.

They offered to pay all expenses for me and a family member of my choice, and provided appealing pictures of the hotels and recreation opportunities.

I was immediately given the understanding that their true intention was to kidnap me as soon as I arrived, get all the information out of me that they could, hold me for ransom, and would then brutally assault and decapitate me.

The conference desk that I saw I would be sitting at was the very desk that was run and operated by the Rothschild family, who are some of the puppet masters behind the New World Order. Despite all the appearance of being a friendly email, I completely ignored it.

At the same time I was receiving the threatening messages, I was visited by evil spirits who were making it clear to me that they were going to stop me from moving forward with the relief effort, and that I had better comply. The adversary clearly wasn't happy I had seen through their puppets' efforts on their last email.

Two weeks later I received a threatening email with a picture of a man, saying in effect, it was his personal vendetta to "destroy me and anyone in my organization if I continued to move forward."

At that time, I hadn't told a living soul of my intentions to create a charitable organization, not even my husband. I had learned all too well by then that opposition like that meant I was on an inspired path, those adversarial attempts to thwart me dispelled all fear and any doubts I was having about it being an inspired decision provided the incentive for me to push harder and get the organization formed as soon as possible.

As an empath, or one who is prone to feel the negative emotions that are constantly being sent my way, the extreme negativity eventually caught up with me which caused my Lyme auto-immune diseases to flare up. I was bed ridden for about a week.

There was a lunar eclipse on September 27th, and on September 28th and 29th I slipped into another near-death experience, exactly eleven years from my September 2004 near-death experience.

While my struggle was less severe, it became a pivotal experience. Through it I came to realize more significantly the importance of my mission, and that people need to press forward with faith in Christ, relying on Him, and that no matter what people say about me, I know what I know!

When I awoke I was given the message: "This is the 11th anniversary of your 2004 near-death experience; we are in the eleventh hour before the Lord's second coming."

I was also given the understanding that there would be another significant event in the heavens in the future. I was shown the book of Revelation, chapter 12 by John the Revelator, who describes the 13 planets aligning, which event happened for the first time in 7,000 years on September 23, 2017, and which signified the 13th anniversary of my 2004 near-death experience.

Through those near-death experiences I was shown that I would be the founder of a relief organization in the future. I saw warehouses, weigh-stations, out-buildings, and safe-houses, rescue missions, and the movement of supplies. Reminders of that foresight began to return through impressions and visions in February of 2015 while on my speaking mission. Those reminder experiences brought added insight that I needed to create a formal organization that would 'marshal the troops' so to speak, and which would provide the organizational backbone to put volunteers to work, which I understood would consist of two counseling bodies. It would also provide a legal entity for receiving funds and making expenditures.

I knew the organization name would include the title of my book, *A Greater Tomorrow,* and was given the understanding that I needed to continue on with my speaking mission, but that the details of establishing the organization would come in August when I concluded that phase of my mission.

Following the lunar eclipse and my revelatory out of body experience, a man by the name of Terry who was one of the attendees of my St. George speaking event was told by the spirit, "Jeff and Julie need your help." He soon contacted me and offered his support, not really knowing how he might do so, other than perhaps helping to start an online charitable funding account.

We started working together and learned that it would be necessary to create a business and incorporate it, which we did on October 20, 2015 and the Greater Tomorrow Relief Fund (GTRF) was established as a 501c3 nonprofit organization. Our work had all been done over the phone, and Terry and I wouldn't meet in person until November when he flew out to Iowa. On that visit we learned that we were distant cousins through my Grandma Hanchett.

Incorporations require board members to run legally, of course, so I chose individuals who showed exemplary interest in providing relief. I asked the Lord why he was having me set up a board when I felt like back in 2008 I had decided I would never go into business with anyone again. The impression came that I wouldn't have to for long, but I would need to at first, then establish counsels. I was told to have faith and trust Him, and that it would all be as it should in time.

In October of 2016, I was feeling the weight of the mission that I was in the process of coming to understand in more detail. In that mindset I began to receive a live feed from the spirit and recorded a chain of vignette's pertaining to my mortal mission, which had a sort of abstract and poetic feel.

I was told to post those vignettes to my blog where all who had access would read, knowing that not all would understand, but those who were meant to understand would be able to interpret their meaning. Little did most of my readers know that I was spelling out major aspects of my mission and details concerning the future. There were a few discerning readers who were able to interpret what I wrote.

Those who did not understand my blog entry took it as evidence that I had lost my mind. With my heightened spiritual senses I immediately began to feel an onslaught of negative emotions and thoughts many of my viewers were having toward me. The weight of their negative emotions caused great spiritual and physical pain—the sort of pain that causes my spirit to detach from my body, causing me to slip into another out of body experience. I was about to face some of the darkest emotions and view some of the darkest situations and places that I had ever encountered.

In one of the more notable experiences, my spirit was carried to the bottom of a deep and dark ocean where I heard and felt the groaning of a familiar voice. I looked to its source at the bottom of the sea floor and saw a man with a millstone around his neck and chains binding his arms and legs to the ground. It was Nick, the man who had stalked and sexually assaulted me over twenty years previously.

He was the one who had abused me as I begged and begged him to stop. Only the tables had now turned. As I confronted my assaulter face to face, he pleaded and pleaded with me to forgive him. "Please don't leave me here," he said, over and over. "I'm so sorry, please don't leave me here." He begged me, like I had begged him to stop all those years ago.

I had already forgiven Nick in my heart years previously, but in that moment, sensing his sheer agony and pitiful misery, I expressed my complete forgiveness to him personally. I was then carried away from that scene as I sensed Nick had been given some measure of relief, but who was still weighed down by his actions with many other abuse victims. I sensed that each of his victims would also need to individually offer their sincere forgiveness in order for Nick to find a true measure of deliverance from his misery.

That experience was heart-wrenching and miserable, but it gave me great spiritual relief. It deepened my sense of the Lord's justice and mercy; His mercy in providing both Nick and I that opportunity for healing and forgiveness; and His justice, knowing that certain sins and their effects can indeed lead to suffering and misery by millstones in a spiritually physical sense, not in the purely metaphoric sense that we often read in the scriptures.

It took me a couple weeks to recover from the difficulty of my health challenges and this experience; but the incident wasn't entirely negative. As with her other near-death experiences I was taught certain doctrines, and given instruction concerning my future mission, which included more about the organization of counsels that needed to be established in my non-profit organization.

I also learned that there were many individuals I had not yet met who the spirit had awakened to a sense of duty and a desire to serve. The next phase of my mission would largely focus on gathering those with a foreordained mission to help and serve their fellow men through my charitable organization. I began to see that a number of small but informal events would need to be arranged to facilitate the gathering of those key individuals.

The first of those events happened in Southeast Idaho during December of 2016. I had seen it in vision and dream for several months, but had the challenge of making it happen with only $245 in the GTRF bank account. I had depleted my personal funds years previously through the speaking events, and was not quite sure how to make the trip.

I knew the trip needed to happen but suspected the GTRF board would not support the use of the corporate credit card without any funds coming in. Two individuals volunteered their time and financial resources to see that the trip would materialize; one of which was on the board at the time. It was determined that when revenue was generated in the future, those individuals would be reimbursed for their expenses. The decision to send me to Idaho and to reimburse any expenses was unanimous. The event was not fruitful in terms of raising funds, as had been hoped, but it was successful in bringing a core group of individuals together; relationships of a deeply eternal nature and historical significance.

One week following the first trip, I sensed another trip was needed, which was how I had seen it for several months. I initially felt some apprehension asking the board to approve yet another trip, which produced no funds, and might seem to them as unimportant. On the other hand, I knew my source of direction, and to me it wasn't the Board of Directors. I fully intended to execute my rights as President of GTRF, and vocalized those intentions to the board.

It was a bold statement that would begin to plant doubts in some of their hearts. Fortunately, the man not on the board who had put forth funds the first time, donated additional resources to make the next trip possible. The board unanimously approved the event as with the first trip, but within a couple days, some of them retracted their votes; an informal action which would carry no legal weight. With the unanimous vote already officially recorded, and as it was meant to be, I boarded a private plane one week later headed to Idaho.

That trip was similar to the first, but cast its net further out on the geographic region, pulling in a number of other contacts made during the speaking events from 2014 and 2015. Nearly 30 people from Idaho, Colorado, Utah, and Arizona met initially as strangers, but a deep sense of familiarity and camaraderie ensued as friendships formed or were strengthened. Tours took place that would familiarize some of the outsiders with the geography and events as they would transpire in the future according to the visuals and insights I had received. As with the first trip, no revenue was generated, but a more spiritual and fundamental foundation became the fruits of the needed trip. Many of those involved had dreams and visions of their own.

In late January of 2017, and still with only $247 in the GTRF bank account, I was directed to hold a meeting in Arizona that would be similar to the previous two Idaho events. I was told that there were a number of contacts in the area that had been made years previously during the speaking events, who needed to be brought together. Those individuals would form foundational relationships for the events that lie ahead in GTRF's future of providing relief in Arizona.

A friend put forth some funding to assist my airfare costs, and another family hosted me in their home over the five day trip. Participants of that visit met and went on a short driving excursion to get acquainted with locations of future events. Some basic organizational planning took place, but the main purpose of the trip was to establish some needed connections.

Following the trip, my hostess sent a text message stating that she enjoyed our time together but it was time to "part ways" with no explanation as to why. Though the news was unpleasant to hear, I had general foresight that such parting would soon be the case, so the change in relationship didn't come as a surprise.

On February 1, 2017, two days following my visit to Arizona, the Vice President of GTRF submitted his letter of resignation, respectfully indicating his high regard for me and belief in my experiences and gifts, along with his hope for a restructuring of the organization.

Two days later two more board members resigned, each expressing belief of my past spiritual experiences and outlining similar hopes for restructuring GTRF. The common thread among the resignations indicated "behind the scenes" collaboration, which discussions I had discerned through the spirit by the time the resignation letters arrived. Again, while not surprising, the rejections wore heavily on my heart.

On the bright side, the reduction in management and opinions on how GTRF should run was a professional relief. It would greatly simplify business in the decisions that lie ahead in the future, and the context of the governing counsels that I had been shown during my last near-death experience begin to make more sense.

The following week I made a trip to Utah, using the funds donated to me personally, so expenditure approval from the GTRF board for the trip was not necessary, even though it would largely be GTRF business I conducted on the trip. I set up appointments with high profile individuals and with no purse or script to work with.

I completed the Utah trip doing a little missionary work along the way. On my flight home I sat next to a Catholic man from St. Mary, Kansas, who had 13 children. Feeling a prompting from the spirit I boldly told him about my near-death experience and the upcoming earthquake that would take place on the Wasatch front. For two hours we shared stories as we were both uplifted and enjoyed each other's company.

For the next several months I focused my efforts mainly on writing my biography, and making an occasional trip as the spirit directed to find more contacts and to bring members of the relief effort together. My biographer and I were told to have the first draft of the book largely completed by March of 2017, not fully understanding why, but suspected a potential spring earthquake along the Wasatch.

As Spring came and went without an earthquake, we both learned that the biography needed to be finished so we could work on the next portion of our mission, to record podcasts together.

Our family in Pomona, Kansas in April 2017. Ethan was 18, Spencer was 16, and Aubrianna was 13.

CHAPTER TWELVE

Hurry Up and Wait

Another spring had sprung without an earthquake along the Wasatch. Every spring and fall since the 2016 Bryan Hyde Radio Talk show felt like it could have been the right time frame, but resulted in another fruitless season. I questioned if what I had been shown would ever happen at times, and yet, I continued to receive impressions that I needed to keep working, holding GTRF meetings, calling individuals on the phone, locating key properties and other GTRF initiatives.

One of those impressions came in May of 2017. My time and attention had largely been occupied by interviews for my biography, but with my book close to completion, thoughts and impressions of creating a podcast became more frequent and I knew the time for the next phase of taking my message to the public had come.

By that time I had spent around 400 hours of recording for my biography, and recognized the natural working relationship I had established over the previous five months with my biographer. Additionally, he and I knew it was part of his mission to be a support and a witness to me and my mission.

I conveyed to him the spirit's recently intensified promptings for creating a podcast, and it was discussed that I had already reached a target audience mainly in the reader community, but that a new audience could be reached through social media outlets. We got to work and within a week of that first conversation, YouTube and PodOmatic stations had been launched, and three episodes were published. At the beginning of the week my station ranked in the three thousand's for popularity and climbed to the number nine spot overall on PodOmatic by the Saturday of that week.

It seemed like heaven had given me a two year reprieve from public appearances, and it was time to ramp up my publicity efforts again. I had been shown previously that my media outreach efforts would begin with books, spread to radio shows, podcasts, a biography, and could eventually evolve to a full feature length documentary.

With each new tier of media outreach I gained new experience and confidence. As an added bonus, my two year break had lead to some measure of healing from some of my health conditions, as I developed a new surge of vitality that was noted by several of my podcast listeners and close associates. While I still had some health struggles, It was as though I had been blessed with a reversal in aging, and an emotional second wind.

I continued to marvel at the way the spirit orchestrated certain events. For example, in May I was told by the spirit I needed to take a trip to Idaho again. I was concerned about my finances and wasn't able to afford the trip. A friend in Idaho offered to purchase my round trip airfare. I was given the dates of the trip several times, and asked repeatedly if I had the correct dates. Feeling confident in my confirmation, I put it on the calendar, booked a plane ticket and made preparations with my hosts.

I used my personal finances to fund my trip. After everything was booked my host told me she was excited to have me stay with them on Father's Day, and that her father would also be staying with them. I gasped! The fact that it would be Father's Day had completely escaped my attention and I was afraid my husband and children would be upset with me for missing a special day together. I began wondering if it was too late to cancel my flight, and it was. But I knew the spirit had confirmed it so I kept my plans.

When Father's Day finally came, my hosts, and their parents, the Gibbys, were having a Sunday barbeque, enjoying each other's company. After talking with Mr. Gibby for some time I learned that he is the owner and operator of a media production company specializing in documentaries.

We hit it off, and after knowing each other for less than two hours I boldly but playfully said to Lon Gibby, "Would you like to do my documentary?"

He responded, "I would be happy to do your documentary." We shared a laugh and immediately launched into strategic planning for the new press effort.

Lon knew little of my background, and hadn't yet read my books, but he had been perfectly prepared to work on such a project; personally as well as professionally. Having had some amazing spiritual experiences himself, combined with his personal devotion to liberty, religious freedom, and his understanding of government corruption and other concerns, he felt a natural connection to me and a drive to tell my story. Neither Lon nor I knew how the documentary would be funded. We pushed forward in faith, trusting the Lord would provide a way.

Two weeks later on July 17, 2017, I was a speaker at a preparedness conference in Rexburg Idaho. Emotions and memories were triggered of standing at the same pulpit almost exactly two years previously in July of 2015, when I gave my last address publicly during my speaking mission. During my speech at the preparedness conference, I gave a heartfelt speech centered on my testimony of the Savior.

As with previous speaking events I would find out within the weeks following why I had really been in attendance at the conference. During the event a number of people greeted me and provided interesting insights and witnesses concerning their own missions or insights they had regarding me and my mission. It took weeks to process all that had happened, but the overall result was a number of new contacts who would become key members of my team.

Years previously I had been given understanding concerning two counsels that would need to be created at some point. Some of the witnesses I had been given at the conference combined with nudges from the spirit in answer to my prayers gave me the confidence that it was time to form the counsels.

My instructions were to form an advisory board for GTRF which would consist of a presidency, a council of fifteen, and a council of 24. This counsel would consist of men and would be focused on rescue missions and tactical related missions. A duplicate advisory board would also be created consisting of women, and would be tasked with gathering and managing supplies like hygiene kits, health and first aid kits, and other physical and spiritual materials that would provide relief in days to come.

About that time, our oldest son Ethan had graduated from high school, got a summer job and began making plans for serving an LDS mission. It was a decision met with mixed emotions for me. For years I had seen in vision my husband and each of our children at what appeared to be the age of my soon departing missionary, and I had never been shown anything concerning his mission.

According to my own timeline, the initial Wasatch earthquake would already have occurred, the LDS church would have stopped calling out missionaries, and we would soon be making preparations for heading west. But I recognized that

I did not always understand the Lord's timing, and continued moving forward, hoping and trusting in the Lord and what he had seen fit to show me.

I had seen many times that my husband would at some point take a new job closer to home and his weekly four hour commute to Iowa would come to an end. Jeff had recently applied for a job closer to home and an offer was made on July 27, 2017, which he readily accepted. The job would be an increase in pay, we would have less expense related to Jeff's commute as well as room and board and best of all, we would have more family time. The same month Jeff was called as the Second Counselor in our ward's bishopric.

Jeff's recent changes weren't the only stars aligning for us. A few weeks later I went on a GTRF trip to Rexburg during the Great American Solar Eclipse. It was interesting to me that the path of totality crossed near my home in Kansas on one end and Rexburg on the other end where I was at the time and which I believe will be my future home.

The darkened period of time while the sun hid behind the moon followed by an outburst of light seemed to signify that period of darkness known as the Tribulations before the glorious return of the Son of God. Additionally, I began anticipating the thirteenth anniversary of my 2004 near death experience which would fall five days after the September 23rd planetary alignment spoken of in Revelation 12 of the New Testament. I understood it to be the first complete planetary alignment in 7,000 years.

Earlier in the month, a M5.3 earthquake and subsequent swarm that went on for months took place in southern Idaho. About the same time a M8.1 earthquake occurred in Mexico and was called by some reports, the "largest in a century."

By the end of the month we saw one of the most intense hurricane season's we've had in decades, destroying hundreds of homes. On October 2, the largest mass shooting in U.S. history since 1949 took place in Las Vegas. It seemed for a time as though natural and man-made events were off the charts.

Several months later in May of 2018 the volcano I visited as a girl in Hawaii began to show unusual activity. Dozens of deep earthquakes in the southwest Pacific preceded the activity, seeming to bring Mt. Kilauea and its neighbor, Pu'u O'o to life.

Within about a month both volcanoes' magma chambers had drained completely and their craters had collapsed. Their contents made way through Hawaiian residential areas destroying hundreds of homes. Ancient volcanoes that hadn't seen activity in hundreds, and in some cases thousands, of years began to stir at the same time. It was as though the earth was awakening from a deep sleep.

Thoughts of my youth trip to the Big Island returned and the recollection that I was told as a young girl that Mt. Kilauea was linked to my mission. I couldn't help but wonder if Kilauea's activity might trigger seismic activity on the mainland, and particularly in the Wasatch region of the Rocky Mountains, where I've been told that future seismic event will occur that is also related to my mission.

As those events were taking place, understanding of my true identity and the role I will complete in the years preceding the Savior's Second Coming following the Wasatch Wakeup became absolute. Although that event hasn't happened yet, I know that it will happen soon. I know that what I have seen will take place in the very near future.

I know that what I have experienced is real and that I have a foreordained mission to help warn others of the days ahead of us. I know that God has a plan for each and every one of us and that it is a plan of happiness. I know this plan of happiness is designed by God to help us learn and grow and become like Him with the hopes of returning to our Heavenly home.

I have seen His plan. I have seen His home. I have felt His heart. I have seen some of our past, present, and future and I believe Him when He tells me we have a bright future. He loves you and He loves me. More than we can even imagine.

I'm grateful for the blessings and gifts the Lord has given me. I'm grateful for the trials and adversities I've experienced which have helped shape my perspectives and believes. I'm grateful for the blessings of the gospel of Jesus Christ which have given me healing and hope and increased capacity to bear the burdens placed upon me.

I'm grateful for truth and knowledge, which have come at a cost, but have been worth every bit of pain, sorrow and suffering. I'm grateful for the atonement of our Savior Jesus Christ,which makes it possible for us to repent, heal and become whole. I'm grateful for the atonement which makes it possible for us to return home. I'm grateful for a loving Father in Heaven who is carefully orchestrating His plan so that we can become like Him.

I'm grateful for the opportunity to share some of my story. My hope is that in reading my story you will come to find greater strength in the Lord, increased capacity to cope, and healing in your hearts. My hope is that you will find a measure of peace you haven't felt before, knowing that God loves you. He is aware of you, He has a plan for you, and He wants you to be happy. My hope is that you too will come to a knowledge and understanding that we have a greater tomorrow. The Lord fulfills all of his promises to his children. This I know.

God bless you and God Speed.

Shalom

Eric J. Smith

ABOUT THE AUTHOR

Eric J. Smith works as a Geographic Information Systems consultant in east Idaho, and has operated his own business since 2009. On the side for a fun change of pace he teaches mapping classes as an Adjunct Faculty member in the History, Geography, and Political Science department of Brigham Young University Idaho.

He received his Bachelor of Science degree in University Studies from BYU Idaho in 2004, and then received his Master of Science degree in Geographic Information Science from Idaho State University in 2013.

For ten years he had a side hobby of mapping cemeteries, bringing a high degree of spatial accuracy to the cemetery mapping industry. His professional life often had a focus on emergency preparedness and disaster mitigation, and he was able to receive training at FEMA's National Emergency Training Center in Maryland with a focus on mapping. In 2016 he was able to combine his personal and professional interests and started a 501c3 charitable organization called Mapping Hands Incorporated, focused on cemetery and disaster relief mapping.

In 2013 Eric experienced a deepened sense of spirituality and closeness with God, and began researching and studying Judeo-Christian doctrines, and studied Biblical Hebrew under Bruce Satterfield at BYU Idaho. About that time he started a blog called "Doctrinal Essays" where he published his research and thoughts on meaningful topics to him.

In 2014 Eric and his wife began reading near-death experience books. Together they found most of them to be authentic, and their depictions of future events and heavenly experiences to be instructive and very touching.

Through those experiences Eric found a passion for writing. In 2016 he teamed up with Spring Creek Book Company as an editor, seeking to gain experience in the writing industry, ultimately leading to writing *Rising Above the Flames* with Julie Rowe in 2017.

Eric loves living in eastern Idaho and his simplistic lifestyle. He enjoys the outdoors with his wife and five children, as well as woodwork, Jazz music, and cooking.

Eric would love to hear from his readers and can be contacted at **Agreatertomorrow2014@gmail.com**

Other Books by Julie Rowe

A Greater Tomorrow

In 2004, Julie Rowe was a happy wife and mother. Then her health took a turn for the worse. While in a weakened state, her spirit left her body and entered the Spirit World. An ancestor named John greeted her and showed her many wonderful places there. He also allowed her to read from the Book of Life, which showed her a panorama of the earth's past, present, and future.

The Time is Now

In this companion volume to her first book, Julie focuses on giving additional details about the future events she was shown, and how we can best prepare for them. Throughout the book, Julie stresses that we must not delay our preparations. These events are not far off, and this book will help you be ready for what awaits us.

From Tragedy to Destiny

A compilation of Julie's first two books, with an emphasis on what awaits America. She was shown that after a period of turmoil, America will rise above these tragedies and fulfill its destiny as a bastion of freedom and liberty.

The Julie Rowe Show Podcast series, with Eric J. Smith

The Julie Rowe Show debuted in 2017 and quickly blossomed into one of the nation's most popular podcasts. Program host Eric J. Smith guided best-selling author Julie Rowe through 60 episodes that covered various aspects of Julie's near-death experiences and what she has been shown regarding future events. Those episodes are now available in this six-volume collection.